LIFE SENTENCE

MURDER VICTIMS AND THEIR FAMILIES

CATHERINE CLEARY

THE ·O'BRIEN PRESS

DUBLIN

First published 2004 by The O'Brien Press Ltd,
20 Victoria Road, Dublin 6, Ireland.
Tel: +353 1 4923333; Fax: +353 1 4922777
E-mail: books@obrien.ie
Website: www.obrien.ie

ISBN: 0-86278-858-7

British Library Cataloguing-in-Publication Data
A catalogue record for this title is available from the British Library

1 2 3 4 5 6 7
04 05 06 07

Typesetting, editing, layout and design: The O'Brien Press Ltd
Printing: AIT Nørhaven A/S, Denmark

DEDICATION

To those who died and those who loved them.

ACKNOWLEDGEMENTS

This book could not have been written without the co-operation of each family who told the story of their own case. It would have been impossible to do justice to those stories without the support, help and encouragement of my family and friends most especially Liam, my parents Joan and Shane and my parents in law Catherine and Benny.

Thanks to Moe Reynolds and Liam Neville of Victim Support for their insights and assistance. Thanks to Paddy Murray, editor of the *Sunday Tribune*, and colleagues in the paper for encouragement and allowing me the time to complete this project.

Thanks are also due to solicitor Michael Finucane of Brophy's solicitors for his help with the chapters on the cases of Joan McCarthy and Sylvia Sheils. Thanks to Paul Allen and to Denis and Mary Murphy for allowing us to reprint Mary's submission to the sentencing hearing for those accused in connection with the death of her son, Brian.

For their help in contacting people in connection with interviews for the book thanks also to David Nally of RTÉ, Conor Lally of the *Irish Times*, Harry McGee of the *Examiner* and Fine Gael Councillor Michael McWee. For their ideas, help and encouragement my thanks to Alison O'Connor, Maol Mhuire Tynan and Mairead Carey. Thanks to Detective Inspector Padraig Kennedy, Detective Inspector Brendan McArdle and Detective Inspector Brian Sherry. And for his insights into the difficulties faced by those bereaved by murder, thanks to clinical psychologist John Donohoe.

Finally thanks to editor Eoin O'Brien and all at O'Brien Press, especially Michael O'Brien for talking me into writing this book in the first place.

Photographs reprinted with the kind permission of the families.

CONTENTS

Introduction

The end of happiness

The mechanics of the aftermath of a murder are predictable. Almost as soon as a heart stops beating after a violent death the State steps in. If you were to be murdered in Ireland tomorrow the State would dictate what happens to your body in the hours that follow. In most circumstances the people who loved you would be unable to do what might come naturally in reaction to a death.

Your loved ones would be unable to lie down with you, to hold you, to breathe in the smell of your hair and your clothes, to kiss your cheek. Such goodbyes, if they come, would happen much later, after the agents of the State are finished their work.

Instead of a quiet end to your life, the room or field or footpath where you died would fill with strangers – people with a job to do, people who have seen this kind of thing dozens of times before. You would be photographed where you were found, and in the way that you were found. No-one would be permitted to fix your clothes or adjust your hair for the camera. Everything in the room or area would be examined. Men and women in white paper suits, tightly drawn hoods and white covers on their shoes would pick over everything you or your murderer touched, sat on, ate, held or otherwise came into contact with.

The material under your nails might be extracted to look for evidence of skin cells you might have scraped from an attacker's body.

The temperature of your body could be taken, to help determine when your death occurred. Later on the mortuary table, your body would be subjected to the investigation of the pathologist's scalpel and weighing scales. More photographs would be taken. Notes made. Evidence gathered.

A bruise or graze you might have suffered days earlier from knocking an elbow off a door, or a shin on a coffee table, would be noted in the post-mortem report. No physical detail would be spared or glossed over. If your hair is dyed the pathologist would note the presence of bleach or colourant in the shaft of your hair.

There is nothing malicious in the actions of the professionals who step in when a murder is committed. Not to examine and record in the way they do would be a dereliction of duty. The procedures are necessary to determine the how, the when and the who of a violent death.

Only when all this work is completed, when every clue your body might have to give has been recorded, would the State step back again to allow your family say goodbye. Your body would now be released for the funeral. Often family members are in a haze of sedation, prescriptions being handed down by family doctors in an effort to carry relatives through the public duties of a funeral.

At the funeral there would inevitably be a large crowd. Reporters and photographers might gather, to record the tributes paid from the altar and photograph the coffin being carried out. The gardaí investigating your murder would probably attend, not only as a mark of respect but also as part of their inquiry if the murderer has not yet been apprehended.

The investigation into your death would occupy the working lives of several dozen people – senior detectives, ordinary gardaí, forensic scientists, scene-of-crime experts, law officers, typists, office clerks and administrators.

Paperwork would begin to pile up, statements and reports all being compiled into the book of evidence. Somebody in the Office of the Director of Public Prosecutions would read through all the material. The decision to prosecute routine cases is made by the Gardaí, but in the case of a murder that decision is made only by the DPP. If the DPP decides not to prosecute the person or people accused of your murder, only the investigating gardaí and those in the DPP's office will know why. The reason is confidential and your family will not be told.

Then months, and in the worst case scenario years, will pass before the murder trial begins. The case would be listed as the DPP versus whoever is charged with the murder. Your name and that of your family would not appear on the court record.

Your family may feel their grief is frozen or stalled in a limbo of waiting. They are waiting for the DPP's decision, waiting for the trial to be given a date, waiting for all the legal teams to be in a position to go ahead.

The morning they walk into the Four Courts, your family would be entering the last arena of Irish public life where cameras are not allowed. Apart from shots of judges lining up on the Supreme Court bench, no still or moving pictures are permitted to be taken in the precincts of the Four Courts when the business of the courts is in session.

This place, that most people won't ever see, can be a bewildering world, like a school or a church in ways, with its bolted-down benches and arcane rules. In the Round Hall of the Four Courts, knots of people would be talking, the ordinary members of the public easily distinguishable from the suited and gowned members of the legal profession. A tipstaff, with a long stick tapping on the floor, and a polite nodding of bewigged heads heralds the arrival of a judge, walking from his or her chambers to a courtroom.

To your family it might appear that everyone knows where they are going and what they are doing. It would seem that even the most junior barrister has perfected an air of authority and knowledge, along with a brisk swing to their robes.

If your family decided to go to Victim Support, they would meet a court volunteer who will help them through the trial. In the courtroom they would see brass plates screwed on benches, with 'bar only' or 'witnesses' written on them. There would be no brass plates to indicate where your family might sit. In the courtroom huge cast-iron radiators pump out heat. If the court were to be full, by the end of the day the room would be stifling.

Busy legal teams would come and go. At times it would inevitably be difficult to hear or understand what was going on. But if they were not treated with 'efficiency, courtesy and fairness', according to the rules laid down in the courts your family could complain to the Courts Service.

Usually the barrister who is to prosecute a murder case would introduce himself or herself to the victim's family, perhaps explain how the case is to be argued and keep in regular contact throughout the trial.

But niceties apart, as far as the system is concerned, your family would have no role here. They would be bystanders, spectators, bunched in with the general public, the relatives of the accused, the groups of school children on tours. The trial would go on in their absence, and there are some legal professionals who would prefer that it did just that. The business of the court is to give the accused person a fair trial.

If that person was on bail they would be entitled to sit in the body of the court, close enough for your family to hear them breathing. The entitlement to the presumption of innocence means that there are no docks in Irish courtrooms. Only the Special Criminal Court has a dock. With its judge-only panel, there is no jury to jump to assumptions because of where the defendant is sitting.

If the defendant is in custody, he or she would sit alongside prison officers, usually on a bench opposite the jury.

In the course of the trial your actions, your reputation and your past behaviour would all be scrutinised by people who never met or knew you. The defence lawyers would earn their fees by trying to persuade a jury that you died for reasons which were beyond the control of their client. As the judge would remind the jury, the job of the defence is not to prove a person's innocence. The job of the prosecution is to prove their guilt, beyond a reasonable doubt.

When the jury finally goes out to consider their verdict, the tension and emotion would be palpable. If a murder conviction is handed down, your family may feel waves of conflicting emotions – relief and emptiness at the same time. The adrenalin that kept them going through the long hours of a trial may have left them drained and exhausted at its close.

After the trial an inquest would be held. If a guilty plea was entered during the trial, your family may have been spared the grisly details of your death. The inquest, designed to ascertain the manner of your death, might therefore hold some horrible information that your family has not heard before.

Finally there will be a death certificate. Someone in your family would have to pay the sum of six euro and ninety-eight cents to a registrar of deaths in order to get the piece of paper recording your death.

This is just one of the documents your family would need in order to apply to the Criminal Injuries Compensation Tribunal. The tribunal needs a Garda report on the crime; financial details for loss of earnings and expenses; funeral expense receipts; details of loss of support or maintenance. The time limit for making a claim is three months, though the tribunal will bend this rule if your family can give a 'reasonable explanation for the delay'.

In 2002 an average of €53,000 per case was paid out by the tribunal. This includes all awards by the compensation tribunal, not just those to the families of murder victims.

Years down the line, maybe when the healing has started for your family, a phone call might come. It might be a priest or a garda. It might be to say that the person who murdered you has been recommended for release. This phone call might only happen if your family requested notification from the Prison Service. Otherwise they might just see the person who killed you in the supermarket or on the pages of a newspaper.

In the year 2002 there was a sad arithmetic to the murder figures. That year Gardaí recorded fifty-two murders, one for every week in the year. In 2003 there were forty-six murders in Ireland.

The repercussions for the families and friends of those who have died are immense. Clinical psychologist John Donohoe has worked with people bereaved by murder, and was instrumental in setting up the Families of Murder Victims group in

Victim Support. The grieving process is different in three broad respects than with a natural death, he says:

Murder expands the circle of grief and shock, he explains. In murder and violent death cases the extended family is considerably affected. The healing process for someone to recover in a normal grieving situation is usually two years, as a rule of thumb. For the death of a child or a suicide that rises to up to six years. In the case of murder, between four and ten years is the average. Most relatives consider that a murder is something from which they never fully recover.

The focus for the grief also provides a huge psychological problem. Instead of finding comfort in remembering how someone lived, thoughts about a murder victim naturally revolve around how they died, who was responsible for that death and the consequences of the murder for the killer.

The third unique element in bereavement through murder is that the legal, medical and media professions, and often the public, can all aggravate the experience of the death for the family.

Medical professionals will sedate and prescribe antidepressants. But grief is not depression, Donohoe argues. Well-meaning people will try to shield a relative from the reality of the murder, advising them not to view the body. For example, May Bishop never saw her daughter Jill after she left the house for a night out on the town with her younger sister. Well-meaning people kept her from saying goodbye and seeing her daughter for a last time.

In such a situation the imagination steps in to fill the gap in knowledge, Donohoe believes. 'The worst realities have limits. Imagination is boundless.' Derek Corbally does not know for certain how his brother Jock died, as his body has never been found. Whatever happened to Jock cannot be worse than the things that Derek has imagined.

Media interest can be a slap in the face as far as a family is concerned. As a reporter, I have taken that walk to the front doors of families after the murder of a loved one. I was fortunate to have worked for newspapers and editors who would accept without question when a family declined to speak. I would like to think that the 'doorstepping' of shocked and bereaved people was an opportunity for those families who did want to speak to paint a picture of their loved one that was true and accurate. Anyone who declined usually did so with astonishing grace and politeness.

The grieving process from a psychological point of view involves the processing of memories, Donohoe believes. A nugget of a memory appears in response to some stimulus and the mind works though it, turning it over like a pebble and then dropping it back in the memory bank. Out of the blue a memory can occur – a smell, a song, a sound, a colour or a touch can bring it to life. As time passes and healing occurs, the processing of memories becomes less painful. In the case of a murder this takes longer; for some people the pain is never fully eased.

The least that people who are living in the shadow of a murder deserve is humanity and kindness from those whose job it is to deal with the aftermath of a violent death. Too often these stories tell of times when this humanity was absent in the response of the State.

Ray Quinn sums up the consequence of his wife's murder in a sentence: for him the murder of his wife Joyce was simply the end of happiness. Sometimes people suddenly realise that they are unhappy, that the colour has left their lives. Generally it is impossible to pinpoint the moment at which their happiness dwindled. For Ray Quinn, it was the exact moment Joyce stopped breathing. Everything from that moment forward has been coloured by her death.

All of the families of murder victims in this book carry the deaths of their loved ones with them. In certain moments the impact is visible. There is a profound sadness, an unsaid and unsayable sense of loss.

Joyce, Aidan, James, Phyllis, Jill, Sylvia, Patrick, Jonathan, Nichola, Jock, Joan and Noel. Six women, four men and two teenage boys, the eldest Sylvia Sheils at fifty-nine, the youngest James Morgan at sixteen.

No-one has been made accountable for the murders of Aidan Gallagher, Sylvia Sheils and Patrick Lawlor. Mystery still surrounds the deaths of Jock Corbally and Joan McCarthy. The men who were convicted in the cases of James Morgan and Noel Neville are both free, having been released after being jailed for the killings. The man accused of Jonathan Edwards' murder was acquitted by a jury.

Four men are behind bars serving life sentences. They are the killers of Joyce Quinn, Phyllis Murphy, Jill Bishop and Nichola Sweeney.

Outside the prisons the families of those who died serve their own form of life sentence. These are their stories.

Chapter 1

It could have been anyone's child

Six years on, she still puts flowers on his grave. Maybe she loved James Morgan from across the classroom. Maybe they kissed. She is one of the blanks in Philomena Morgan's story of her son's short life.

As far as Philomena knows, the girl with the flowers was in the same class as James. Maybe if her son had lived he would have brought her home one day and introduced her to his big family. Philomena is touched by this girl, who has grown into a woman and still leaves a tribute for her teenage love.

The girl is a good blank. There are other blanks – terrible ones, mostly in the last minutes of James Morgan's life – that his parents Philomena and Justin Morgan may never be able to fill in. Why did he get into the car driven by the young milkman Norman Coopey and his accomplice? Did the two men pull over in the heavy summer rain that day and offer him a lift? Or did they grab him and pull him in?

At some stage James told Coopey and the other man his name. This was a crucial detail they had to ascertain before they could bludgeon him to death with a hammer. A wrong name meant the wrong religion. They wanted to kill a Catholic. The fact that James was in a Catholic village was a start, but they had to do a quick name-check to ensure that he was not just passing through. They had to be sure that the rage and hatred that drove them that Thursday afternoon in July 1997 would not lead them to murder the 'wrong' victim.

The house where the Morgan family lives was built two centuries ago by the owners of the linen mills, the economic heart of the area around the small County Down town of Castlewellan. At the end of the town the road plummets down a hill and then climbs up again to the Morgans' home village of Annsborough. Perched on another smaller hill in the village, the two Georgian houses would have been home to the mill managers. Their handsome facades were not quite as grand as the mill owner's mansion, but were more substantial than the workers' cottages.

Justin Morgan, the son of a County Down farmer, works as a builder. He met Philomena who lived in a nearby parish and in 1970 they were married and moved into the house on the hill.

Watched over by the Mourne Mountains, with the highest peak Slieve Donard a towering presence to the east, the countryside seemed to cocoon the family from the daily nightmare of the Troubles. Just a few miles away in the hamlet of Loughinisland, six men were shot dead by UVF gunmen as they drank in a Catholic pub in June 1994. But Annsborough was remote from the riots and murders of Belfast and Derry.

James Morgan slept in the attic room with his brother Jerome. His father Justin converted the attic to accommodate his growing family of six boys and a girl. There was another child – Niall, the baby who was born with a hole in his heart. In February 1978 he underwent heart surgery. He died the following day at the age of two.

James was born more than two years after the terrible loss, on 5 September 1980. He was the second youngest in a home full of dark-haired children. In his sixteen years James had never spent a night away from his parents.

James sat his GCSEs in the summer of 1997, at St Malachy's High School in Castlewellan. His older brother Joseph sat his A-levels at the same time.

James then spent that summer working with his father on building work in the nearby seaside town of Newcastle. Some nights James worked as a waiter in the Slieve Donard Hotel in Newcastle, earning pocket money for clothes and discos. One day the singer Daniel O'Donnell was photographed with James and another young waiter for the local paper. The caption called James and his friend 'Daniel's Youngest Fans'.

Sectarianism was as alien a concept to James as it might have been to any teenager living in a southern village. The fact that one of his best friends – Nathan Elliott – was not a Catholic was nothing remarkable in the small village where people just got on with each other.

It made it all the more unusual as the family drove out of the town on Saturday, 5 July 1997, to see a group of young men gathering to protest about an Orange march that had been due to go through the town. Justin and Philomena had packed up the car to take their two youngest boys on holiday to Kerry. By now the family trip to Killarney in July was something of an annual pilgrimage. It coincided with the marching season but that was not deliberate. As far as they were concerned there was no reason for the family to have to get away.

As they drove out of town that year, one of the boys – Justin thinks it may have been James – looked out the back window of the family car at the angry protesters and remarked to his parents, 'Someone's going to get killed before this is all over.'

In the holiday home in Killarney, they tuned in like the rest of the country to the pictures of celebrations on the streets of Northern Ireland. The IRA had just declared their second ceasefire. It was a time of hope, with talk of seismic shifts and a peaceful future for the children of a generation who had only known conflict.

The Morgan family's two weeks in Kerry ended on a high note with a wedding in Tralee. A cousin of James's was marrying a girl from Tralee and the wedding was a great occasion. A photograph from that night shows James grinning at the camera, dressed in a smart check shirt, one hand on his hip and the other arm around his cousin Trina, the groom's sister. His summer outdoors helping his dad on the buildings is written in his healthy tan in the snapshot. The next day the Morgans made the long drive back to Annsborough.

They stayed in holiday mode even after they got back to the house, slowly getting themselves back into the routine of work. On Thursday, 24 July, Justin and Philomena were getting ready to visit the family of Philomena's aunt Mary who had died while they had been away. Ten minutes before they left the house, at around 2.10pm, James went out to walk up to his friend Nathan Elliott's house. He had not been out of his bed long at that stage, having been out the night before with Nathan.

Dressed in white tracksuit pants and a grey top, James walked out the front door, through his parents' flower-filled front garden and up to the corner. There he would usually have clambered up over the old stone wall, a shortcut to the Elliotts' bungalow saving him the longer walk up the steep hill towards Ardnabannon.

Maybe he took a lift. But his mother does not think so. The lift would have been for just 500 yards – up to the Elliotts' house. With the heavy rain that July day there was no-one around to see what happened.

In the annals of the Troubles, James Morgan is recorded as the boy who was murdered when he was picked up hitch-hiking one night. The hazy details of his disappearance carried in initial media reports have become the version of his death that is repeated whenever his murder is mentioned. The more shocking truth is that James was picked up in the middle of the day at the side of the road just yards from the house where he had lived all his life. He never made it to Nathan's, and his friend went off to Dublin not knowing that James was missing.

Nathan was not the only one who did not realise what had happened to James. That night his parents thought he had stayed in his friend's house or come home when they were out with Philomena's family and retired to his room, climbing the steep stairs to the attic bedroom. The next morning Philomena left for work at 6.30am and Justin went out to start work on building a wall, getting himself back into a work routine after the holiday.

When she returned, Philomena asked her husband why James was not helping him. Justin said he thought the boy might still be in bed. When she checked the room it was empty.

They walked down to the Elliotts' to check if James was there. There was no sign of him. Philomena and Justin figured that he had missed Nathan and gone on to Newcastle to see other friends. While they were out an RUC detective called to their door back home. Their son Joseph answered it. 'Is there anybody missing?' the detective asked him, without saying why he was asking such a strange question. Joseph told the policeman that his parents were away looking for James, but that he was not, as far as they were concerned, missing.

'That's awful strange,' Philomena thought when her son told her about the visit from the police, starting to feel bubbles of anxiety rising. 'Why would a detective be coming looking – and right enough we can't find James.'

They decided to ring Nathan in Dublin to see if James had travelled down with him. Nathan told them he had not seen his young friend. Then there came another knock on the door. It was the police again. They asked about James but would not tell the Morgans why. The police seemed to know something but the officers were giving nothing away. There were still friends in Newcastle to be checked and Justin and Philomena spent the night frantically contacting and visiting everyone they thought might know where he was.

It was those hours, when his son was missing, that Justin Morgan remembers as the worst torture. He says he would not wish on anyone the anguish of a missing loved one. The blank-faced police officers and their questions about what James had been wearing when they last saw him, and now James's unexplained absence, all pointed to one horrible conclusion.

Afterwards they pieced together what had led the police to their door before they even knew their son was missing. Norman Coopey, a man the Morgans had never met, got out of bed that Friday morning and did his milk round as normal. Calling to a cousin of Justin Morgan's at around three o'clock he picked up his milk money and told her he would see her as usual the following week. Only he and one other man knew what he had done in the previous twenty-four hours. With his ordinary day's work done, Norman Coopey then did an extraordinary thing. He walked into Newcastle police station and started talking.

What he told the police left them shaking their heads in disbelief – here was a man in off the street confessing to a murder that he had just committed. He gave them everything – the name of his victim, how they killed him and where they dumped his body. In that first statement he even named the other man who had attacked the schoolboy. That man has never been charged with the murder, for lack of evidence.

The police could not tell James's parents the story that Coopey had relayed to them until they were sure it was true. Unknown to the Morgans, their son's murderer's statement was already written up on police paper and would later go into the book of evidence for the prosecution against him.

When the police called to the door, more than twenty-four hours after the Morgans had last seen James, the officers had no way of knowing whether what Coopey had told them was just the delusional thoughts of a madman or matters of fact. They had to find the family of this James Morgan that a milkman was telling them had just been murdered. When they got there Justin and Philomena were just beginning to realise that James was gone.

At lunchtime the next day, Saturday, the detectives called back to the house and said they were starting to dig. They had cordoned off an area of farmland four miles from the Morgans' front door. At Blackstaff near Clough, the farm was now swarming with police men and women. The Morgans asked the police what they were looking for. The police played it down. That evening Justin drove to the farm and tried to walk down the laneway to see what was happening. A policeman stopped him, but he was close enough to see the white tent, police equipment for protecting a body and any forensic evidence from the weather.

Justin knew from the gentle way the policeman talked to him that James was probably dead. If the police did not know that he was now the father of a murder victim they would have moved him out of the area pretty unceremoniously, he reasoned.

It was later that day that the worst was confirmed. As the Morgans sat in the house waiting for news, the television screen in the corner showed a hearse pulling slowly out of the rutted laneway just five miles away. A police officer and the parish priest were on their way to the house to tell them the news, but the television told it first.

The body in the coffin bore little resemblance to the smiling son Justin and Philomena had seen two days earlier. Coopey and his friend murdered James with a hammer. Coopey told police they beat him with the hammer in the car, dumped his body in the boot and then Coopey 'finished him off' at the farm. They hit him in the face with it, shattering his cheek-bone. Another blow caved in his skull, killing him instantly. Coopey said he kicked the body into a muddy pit where animal carcasses were dumped. They had already doused it in petrol and set it alight.

Some months later Philomena would sit down and read through the clinical description of her son's fatal injuries. It was something she felt she had to do. Justin has never read it and does not let himself think about the manner of his son's death. There is some small comfort in the post mortem report, which came to them via a solicitor's office. When Justin picked it up and brought it home to his wife, Philomena went up to the church and read it in the presence of the local curate. It concluded that James probably died quickly. What they do not know is how long he lived after they lifted him from the side of the road, and whether he knew that he would die. It is another blank.

Nobody other than the murderers and the police saw his body. A small hole was cut in the body bag so that the Morgans' parish priest could anoint his remains with oil. It was not until weeks later that his parents discovered that Coopey and the other man had burned James's body. At the time they were just told that James had been badly beaten. The police took blood samples from them for DNA profiling but, as one detective put it to Philomena, there was none of James's blood left to compare. His blood had been cooked, the officer told her. Dental records had to be used to confirm that the body was their son.

Annsborough and Castlewellan came to a standstill the day of James Morgan's funeral. Father Finbar Galvin told the congregation of more than a thousand people that James had been killed for no other reason than his religion. His message to the congregation was that anyone who supported religious hatred had the schoolboy's blood on their hand. 'Sectarianism is not a licence to kill. God commanded "Thou shalt not kill,"' Father Galvin said. 'He did not say "It's all right if you kick with the other foot." Murder is murder.'

Justin and Philomena sat with their daughter and five other sons, numb with shock. The small village shared their shock. For weeks afterwards parents kept their children close, terrified that what had happened to James could happen again. Rumours of suspicious cars roaming the area spread on a daily basis. School children in James's school were traumatised not just by the death of a fellow teenager, but also by the thought that it could have been any boy, anyone's son, who had been unlucky enough to be out the day that Coopey and his friend came looking for a victim.

In the days and weeks that followed, Justin would find himself just sitting on the couch for hours on end. His life had boiled down to a hollow existence – dressing in the morning, eating without tasting, all of it in a daze. 'There is no hatred in this house and in most of the people in Northern Ireland. There are head cases out there. The mothers and fathers of the people that have done this must be feeling this as well. Nothing makes sense any more,' he told one reporter at the time. When he looks back now, he remembers one morning that the postman called and bills dropped through the letterbox. He roused himself. There was a mortgage to be paid and life was passing by his front window every day.

Despite the fact that life as he knew it had stopped the moment James was murdered, and despite all the sympathy surrounding the Morgans, the ordinary business of living had to continue.

Philomena too carried on looking after her large family, drawing on her deepest reserves of strength. Her grief took on a different shape to Justin's. She mourned her son, but she was also gripped with a determination to see the face of the man who had killed him. She needed to get a picture of the murderer, to see what kind of man would be capable of beating a schoolboy to death and then burning his body. Coopey must have known his victim was just a boy, she believes. Although James was tall for his age, he was slight. His teenage growth spurt had lengthened his limbs, but later years would have filled him out.

At Armagh Crown Court some days after the murder, she waited with Justin and their youngest son Jerome for Coopey to appear. Family, friends and neighbours had packed out the court. As they sat waiting for him to come up from the holding cell for the brief hearing, she was determined to take a good hard look at him as he walked up the steps to the dock.

When he did she was shocked. She found it hard to believe that someone that she now saw as thin and pathetic could be the monster who killed James. She expected a thug with huge arms and a broad chest. Coopey was a figure without physical menace, his smallness emphasised by the bulky prison officers. His features are still clearly imprinted in her mind.

Coopey did not return her gaze. Instead he stared hard at Jerome. Philomena believes her youngest son's face – so similar to his dead brother's – must have jolted Coopey as he prepared to plead not guilty to the murder. That day Philomena felt Coopey wore an arrogant mask of indifference in the court. Only she noticed his jolt of recognition when he saw her son. By the next court appearance he had changed his plea to guilty. She still wonders if the sight of Jerome, a living reminder of the face of his victim, influenced his change of plea.

There is another imponderable blank for the Morgans. What made Coopey walk into the police station and make his statement? Without his confession it was possible that James would never have been found. The lime in the cattle pit would have worked to dissolve his remains, leaving just bones mingled with those of the animals. As a teenage boy apparently gone missing, his case would have been far from a priority for the police. In a hierarchy of concern, younger children and women would always be a more immediate priority. He could have lain in the boggy earth, just four miles from his home, without anyone ever finding him.

There was no apparent reason for the milkman to tell the police anything. Coopey and his accomplice had covered their tracks. They had hosed the blood out of the car boot and burnt their clothes, so any forensic trace of their victim would be destroyed. The bungalows that lined the road to the farm at Clough were empty, their occupants away on holiday the day they drove him down there. In the teeming July rain no-one had seen them pick up their victim, and on the lonely country road no-one had seen them driving down the lane to the cattle pit. After he confessed, the police found traces of blood in the car, but they would never have looked for them there had Coopey not walked into Newcastle police station and started talking.

On 10 January 1999, Coopey was convicted of James Morgan's murder at a sitting of Belfast Crown Court in Armagh. Coopey's defence team said Coopey had been 'very much in fear of the person with him' and that his partner in the crime had attacked James first with a claw hammer he had in the car after they were told his name and religion. Coopey then finished him off with further blows to the back of his head, the court heard.

Lord Justice McCollum described the killing as the heinous murder of a sixteen-year-old schoolboy who was a completely innocent victim of a sectarian attack.

Coopey received the mandatory life sentence and returned in a prison van to the Maze Prison, where he was by then an inmate on the Loyalist Volunteer Force (LVF) wing.

Coopey had been transferred to the Maze after he was beaten up in Maghaberry Prison and rejected by mainstream loyalists. The loyalist terror leader Billy Wright took him in to the LVF wing and in December 1997 Coopey witnessed Wright's murder by the INLA. The milkman was watching from his cell overlooking the yard as Wright was shot dead. He later told Wright's inquest that he saw three men with handguns around the white minibus and watched Wright at the door kicking out at them. After four or five shots rang out Coopey saw Wright fall back into the van.

The move to the LVF wing proved to be Coopey's ticket to freedom. On 28 July 2000, just over three years after the day he murdered James Morgan, Coopey walked out of the Maze a free man. Under the Belfast Agreement, prisoners aligned to any organisation on ceasefire qualified for early release. Coopey had served just eighteen months of his life sentence from the date of his conviction.

In Annsborough, Philomena watched the television in horror as the cameras recorded the releases, one of the last under the agreement. As the reporter described Coopey's crime, the camera focused on a man walking out. It wasn't Norman Coopey. It was a bigger man.

Now and again the Morgans hear news of where Coopey is living. He is in the general vicinity, although they have not set eyes on him. Philomena does not dread seeing him; she does not let herself think about him. If she does pass him in the street or on a road some day, she is not sure what her reaction will be.

The second man that the Morgans believe took part in the killing also lives in the area. Their son is gone and his killers are free.

Like the details of his son's murder, Justin does not allow himself to dwell on the two young men who took James away from them. That way lies madness.

Bereavement counselling was provided for the Morgans, arranged by staff at St Malachy's, the school where James had been a pupil. Philomena and Justin, along with Jerome, would drive to the early-morning sessions and sit together in a room trying to talk about the impact of the murder on their lives. Although the counsellors were kind, the sessions were fruitless. In the presence of his wife and youngest son, Justin felt that he could not say what he might have said about James for fear of upsetting them. As a young teenager Jerome was not at his most forthcoming first thing in the morning.

In August, just weeks after his death, James's GCSE results came through. He had done his parents proud, and would have been more than qualified to go on to A-levels. Joseph, who also sat his exams that year, also did well, and went on to graduate from Queen's University in Belfast.

Later that year a teacher dropped in a photograph of James, that James himself had never seen. It showed him smiling and holding a polished wooden drawer and shelf set, his own work for his GCSE project. The woodwork project now sits on the sideboard with a framed picture of him holding it on top.

Philomena kept his school blazer and the smart check shirt he wore that summer. She gave away his good jumpers to anyone who wanted them and the rest of his clothes went to charity. In the years that followed the murder their busy, noisy family house emptied. One by one the boys moved away. In 2001 their only daughter Roisin got married. Justin expected it to be a tough day without James. In the end it was as happy as it could have been.

Justin Morgan is a different person now, he says. Although he does not carry James's death visibly on his shoulders there is a quiet part of him that will always mourn the boy. He has lost his son to murder but, in so far as everyday obligations and routine go, his life is normal. For both Justin and Philomena, James is always there in the background.

Father Brian D'Arcy introduced them to a former priest, a

bereavement specialist who ran a day-long seminar shortly after James's death. The Morgans were feeling at their lowest point and they see that day as a turning point. They remember the day as a moment of huge emotional release – they managed to laugh and cry. The seminar helped them to remember not the murder and those awful blanks, but James's life and the happy sixteen years they shared with him. They have the comfort of knowing they had done nothing wrong; no-one could blame them for the death of their son.

Justin wonders at the resilience that keeps them going. If it had happened to the man next door to them, he says he would not be able to understand how he could continue. When it happened to them something else took over and life went on.

Justin plays the keyboards and travels around the North for music events. It is at these events that people come up and sympathise with him as the father of the schoolboy who was murdered. Around his village there are people who have forgotten about it.

Letters from strangers flooded through their door after James's murder. An article in the *Sunday Tribune* by journalist Susan McKay, illustrated with a photograph of James taken outside the house on his first day at school, prompted a huge outpouring of sympathy from around the country.

James was shown in the photograph aged just five, standing proudly with his mother's geraniums in full bloom above him on the windowsill as he prepared for his first big trip to school. It is a picture, as his father says, that would touch the heart of anyone. The photograph was flashed up on TV screens around the North after the trial and then the camera showed a catalogue of pictures of James, from his baby pictures to him as a teenager looming tall in the back of family portraits.

The letters kept coming, most of them from strangers moved to write to the family after being so shocked by the murder. Some of the letters spoke of their own tragedies, like losing a child to suicide. One letter stood out. Wexford mother Susan Kirwan wrote a long letter, struck by the fact that her own son James was the same age as the Morgans' boy. 'You are lucky to be the parents of James and not the parents of his killers,' she wrote. The Morgans have visited her in Wexford and the two families have become friends.

There is a community of shared loss in the North, where the murder rate associated with the Troubles has been so high. Other families who lost members have been in contact with the Morgans.

This contact has been a huge support. For the families of murder victims it is sometimes only other people who have gone through the same extraordinary trauma who can say the right thing. And sometimes they are the only ones who know when to say nothing.

James is buried in the cemetery at Aughlisnafin alongside baby Niall, the older brother he never knew. 'Niall died 3rd February 1978 aged two years,' the smart granite headstone reads. 'Also his brother James murdered 24th July 1997 aged 16 years an innocent victim of the troubles.'

Chapter 2
She was everybody's child

'There's my little family,' Ciaran Bishop says proudly, pointing out the black-and-white photograph on his sitting room wall. There are the two smiling girls and their big brother with their parents, Ciaran and May, all walking towards the camera.

The housing estate in the picture has a new look, with freshly painted white houses and a new footpath. Ciaran and May are both still dark-haired. It is a snapshot of hope and promise. The saplings in front of the new houses are now all mature trees in the Corke Abbey estate in Bray, County Wicklow.

Until they sat down and talked it over, Ciaran and May had struggled to answer every time someone asked how many they had in their family. They stumbled over this staple bit of small talk among people meeting for the first time. Now the answer is simple.

'We have three in our family,' they will say. 'John is the eldest. Our eldest daughter Jill was murdered when she was eighteen, and we have Karen.'

'Will that not upset people?' May wondered as they decided on the answer.

'I don't care if it upsets people,' Ciaran insisted. 'We can't say there's two, because that's wrong.'

Out of the blue, May turned to Ciaran at around 3.30 in the morning on Friday, 1 November 1991, and voiced the terrible thought that had just come into her head. 'Jill's been murdered,' she said.

'You can't say that. Don't be so stupid,' Ciaran told her. He had dropped Jill off earlier that night at Jim Doyle's pub in Bray town for a night out with friends.

They were worried. Their eighteen-year-old daughter, who had never spent a night away from home, had not returned as expected. 'I'm telling you she's been murdered,' May said.

In Corke Abbey everyone knew Jill Bishop. The Bray housing estate was full of young couples with children and she was the babysitter everyone wanted. She would be booked up well in advance. Even as a young teenager she was trusted to mind small children. As Ciaran would walk through the estate with his curly-haired daughter, people in cars would beep and wave. 'Who's that?' Ciaran used to ask. Jill would know all their names from looking after their children. In one home she was an honorary family member.

It is a cliché, Ciaran knows, to speak of a murder victim as a special person, but Jill had an effortless ability to make people like her.

After a school trip to Dublin once, she returned with a copy of a Walter Osbourne painting for her dad. 'To Daddy, I hope you like this card, love Jill,' she wrote on the back. She was Jill from very early on. Ciaran's father could never get his tongue around Gillian. The soft 'g' would defeat him and he would call her Gilligan. 'Just call her Jill,' her grandmother would say.

As a child Jill suffered from rheumatoid arthritis, a painful condition that involved lots of time in bed and plenty of hospital visits. It may have been because she was a sick child who spent a lot of time at home, but for whatever reason there was an almost symbiotic relationship between Jill and her mother. May would often hear her daughter laughing as she came up the road. There would be a tap on the window of the front room and May would open the front door.

Friends would tease her that she never stayed overnight because her mother was not there to plump up her pillows and make her comfortable. Jill still enjoyed the comfort of her mother tucking her in to bed before she turned over and went to sleep.

Jill was a giggler and a mimic. If she came home in the evening and her parents were in bed, she would sit on the edge of the bed chatting, talking through everything that had happened and everyone she had met since leaving the house that morning.

If Ciaran objected he would get a pillow in the face or the blankets pulled up over his head while Jill chatted on.

As a teenager she had never gone through the surly phase where parents became the enemy. Every time she left them she would throw her arms around both parents and give them a kiss. There would be the same greeting the next time she saw them, even if only an hour had passed.

At the Carlisle Grounds where Ciaran went to watch football, he would be half embarrassed and half chuffed when Jill gave him her signature greeting.

As his job with the League of Credit Unions meant numerous late nights, he always made a point of driving the kids to school in the morning. Jill's goodbye ritual every day involved going around the car, opening the driver's door and giving him a bear hug.

Now he is grateful that he made a point of being with his kids on those early-morning trips.

Straight out of school, Jill got her first job on the reception desk at the RDS, and she loved it. She was the most junior person in the office, but pretty soon she was talking like she ran the place.

An Italian opera company had done a runner from the venue, failing to pay a bill after a big concert. 'Heads will roll,' Jill told her parents solemnly, relaying the news with all the gravitas of a teenager taking her first steps in the world of business.

That Halloween night in 1991 was wild, a stormy night with wind and rain. Jill's friends wanted her to go to Dublin for a night out, but she was taking her sixteen-year-old sister Karen out to her first disco and thought the city would be too rough.

She came home from work and changed for the night out, taking off her glasses and proudly putting in her new contact lenses. She dressed carefully before asking her mum for a tenner. May put her foot down – she had lent Jill many tenners before, and it was time to pay them back. When Ciaran arrived home he gave his daughter the money.

That simple act would haunt him afterwards, but he knows that May would eventually have given in. She was simply making a point by refusing the first time.

He dropped Jill into the town outside Jim Doyle's pub, where she was meeting friends. As ever, there was the hug and the kiss goodbye. Later he dropped Karen up to meet her.

That night Karen came home alone. Jill was still with her gang of friends, just sending her baby sister home that bit earlier.

By 3.30 in the morning, whether through some kind of maternal connecting force or just from fearing the worst, May Bishop was adamant that her daughter was dead. It was around that time, according to the estimated time of death, that a local man Jill had never met before forced a pound coin down her airway, suffocating her to death.

Ciaran's role as the Dad, the Boss, the man who could mend it or get it mended, went into overdrive that Friday morning when Jill was missing. They found out before the gardaí did that Jill had last been seen in the company of Michael Dean McLoughlin, an unemployed twenty-two-year-old chef she had met at the disco.

The whole family were out looking for Jill. Ciaran kept repeating that there had to be a logical explanation – she was hurt; she had blacked out; she had lost her memory. Whatever had happened could be fixed and he was the man to fix it. That was his role. In his happy little family, May was the nurturer and he was the fixer. Until that morning, that is. With the discovery of his daughter's body, Ciaran felt he could never fix anything again.

He drove down to the seafront. When he got out of the car his legs started to shake. Gardaí were converging on Montebello House, a seafront property with a yard. Everything was happening too quickly. The flurry of activity could not mean anything positive and the commotion was drawing a crowd. When Ciaran went to see what was happening, they pushed him into a squad car. They were kind in a way, but they dismissed him, telling him to stay out of the way. But I'm the dad here, Ciaran thought angrily.

His brother Charlie walked into the house Jill had been dragged into and identified her. McLoughlin had taken her from the Bray Head Hotel up the seafront to the house. He gave her a severe beating on the road. During the attack he forced a pound coin down her throat to stop her screaming.

The post mortem would later record the cause of death as asphyxiation. He stripped her, but did not rape her. He left her body covered in plastic sheeting in the yard at the back of the empty house.

Ciaran felt his control over events slip. He was told not to see her, that her body had already been identified. Then he had to go home to Corke Abbey and tell May. When he got there the house was heaving with people. He could see May across the room and he could see that she already knew, but he couldn't get to her through the sea of people. They couldn't be alone together to try and talk about the awful news, or to just hold each other.

It was as if he was watching events in which he had no part. Now he looks back and thinks that the people who were there, no matter how well-intentioned, in some way wanted a piece of the action, to be part of the drama that was unfolding.

The kindnesses of friends and neighbours took over the ordinary tasks of the day. The doorbell rang and food arrived. Washing up was done, sometimes by people Ciaran didn't even know. Waves of people arrived serving tea. In the surreal aftermath he would find himself accepting cups of tea in his own house from people that he barely knew. At one stage he had to get out, going down to the strand just to feel able to breathe again.

It was during this stage that Ciaran made a mistake that he bitterly regrets more than a decade later.

In a sense everyone becomes an expert when there's been a murder. And in the shock and bewilderment that followed Jill's murder all the experts were all in agreement about one thing. No matter how much she wanted to, May Bishop should not see Jill's body, they said.

Ciaran did see his daughter. At the morgue at Loughlin-stown Hospital he said his goodbye. Later, when the father of one of the Lockerbie victims talked about not having been able to say goodbye to his daughter as there was no body recovered, it resonated with him.

May should have been able to touch her hand, her foot, any part of her, he believes now. That final farewell never happened, and for years his wife waited to hear the knock on the living-room window that preceded Jill bursting through the front door with the day's news. As far as Ciaran is concerned, no one is expert enough to tell a mother not to see her child for the last time if that is her wish.

A few days after the funeral, a man who lived on the estate, whom Ciaran knew to see, called to the door. A very tall Englishman, he had never spoken to the Bishops and kept very much to himself. He said he wanted to tell them a story about Jill.

He worked nights and he told Ciaran that every morning as he returned from work he would meet Jill on her way out of the estate. She never let him pass by without giving him a cheery, 'Hello, how are you.' It became almost a war of attrition. And Jill won. Eventually the man who spoke to no-one began to return her early-morning greeting.

In addition to all the other things they had to deal with in the aftermath of the murder, the rumour mill was an unexpected and unpleasant sideshow. A work colleague told Ciaran that she had heard Jill was murdered by her fiancé after a row. The rumour had it that she was engaged to McLoughlin, when in fact she had only just met him.

A friend of Ciaran's sympathised with him about how awful it was that Jill had gone off with a group of lads. When Ciaran asked, 'What lads?' the friend said, 'You probably haven't heard,' before relaying the rumour as if it was gospel.

Then people began to talk about the pound coin. The horrible news reached Ciaran and May. 'That's not true,' Ciaran said repeatedly. Eventually a member of the Garda murder squad told him that it was indeed the case. The coin had been discovered during the post mortem. Somebody somewhere had talked about it, and the Bishops heard it from the rumour mill before they were officially told.

At his local pub the punters would offer to buy Ciaran a drink whenever he was in. It was partly sympathy but also curiosity. And some nights if he wasn't there, his best friend Larry would be pumped for information.

There was a mixture of morbid fascination and genuine sympathy. At one stage an unfortunate man got tongue-twisted as he offered his sympathy. Ciaran and May met him on the street. 'It couldn't have happened to a better family,' the poor man said, nerves getting the better of his good intentions. They knew that what he meant to say was that it should never have happened to a family like theirs. Afterwards they could only laugh.

Nothing was the same after the murder. And there were practical as well as emotional consequences. Although his day job was in helping others to manage their finances, Ciaran lost the run of his own. Being careful with money no longer seemed a priority. The future was an abstract blur rather than a hard financial reality. The Bishops were spending like there was no tomorrow, because, in the aftermath of the murder, there was no tomorrow.

Eventually the inevitable letter came from the bank manager and Ciaran was furious. In a rage he drove to Bray town and parked in the Holy Redeemer Church car park. He talked to his daughter all the way down. 'If this fucker gives me grief today I'm not going to take it,' he told her. 'And you'd better do something about it.'

Ready to do battle with a hard-faced pencil pusher, he instead met a man he remembers as one of the nicest guys in the banking business. 'We've got to sort you out,' the bank manager told him. Ciaran walked out as if he had been given money, although all he had agreed was a repayment plan. He thinks Jill had a hand in organising a friendly face at the other side of the desk.

Other encounters were not so positive. At their first counselling session, the first question Ciaran and May were asked was whether they could forgive Jill's murderer. They turned and left the counsellor's office.

Another counsellor provided much more therapeutic sessions, but then she went on leave and their case was transferred. Before she left she did manage to get the post mortem report for them. May always wanted to see the report, to read in cold, clinical detail how her daughter died.

The counsellor left them in the room with the typed report for half an hour. When she returned she told them the copy of the report was theirs to keep. May shook her head. She wanted to read the information, but she did not want to keep it or to take the pages home. The task was done and they left the typed report behind. She did not want it in the house.

The grief of losing a child made any other bereavement pale in comparison. Ciaran had lost both his parents and grieved for them. But when Jill died it was a whole other dimension of loss.

In her book *Homicide: The Hidden Victims*, Deborah Spungen, whose daughter Nancy was allegedly stabbed to death by Sid Vicious, calls the families of murder victims the 'co-victims'. She points out that there is no word in the English language for a parent whose child has died. A person who loses their parents is an orphan. There are widows and widowers. There is no term to describe the brokenness a parent feels following the death of a child.

The death of a child goes against the natural order of things. A parent's role in the world is to protect their children, and a parent who buries a child has their world blasted apart. The pieces never fit together the same way.

The Bishops mourned a life unlived. As Jill's friends grew up around them, they were reminders of the steps Jill never took.

The friends have kept in touch. When Jill's best friend Hazel Cullen got married the Bishops were invited to the wedding. However, they felt it would be too hard to be there and did not go. The father of the bride referred to Jill in his speech as having been like a member of their family.

Hazel and other friends used to visit May regularly. There would be chats around the kitchen table about boyfriends, engagements, work and life in general. She has watched her daughter's friends grow from teenagers to young women and young mothers. Her delight at their visits was always followed by sadness.

Ordinary happy family events became fraught with extraordinary worry. When Karen was nearing her twenty-first birthday, her parents discussed endlessly whether they would throw a party for her. Even though Jill was only eighteen when she died, she had already started to talk about her plans for a twenty-first.

Karen's birthday was an event that would be littered with emotional landmines. If they celebrated their youngest daughter's step into adulthood, the festivities might be over-shadowed by Jill's absence and a birthday never celebrated.

As it turned out, it was the best party they had ever thrown. It was as if everyone went with the intention of making it a night to remember.

After she blew out the candles, Karen's friends called on her to make a speech. Ciaran felt the blood drain from his face, wondering how she would cope at such an emotional moment. But she did a brilliant job. She said all the right things.

When he looks back now, twelve years later, Ciaran wonders how John and Karen coped with the loss. All the support was directed towards himself and May, as the parents of the dead girl. People would arrive at the house and immediately reach for the adults in the room to sympathise with and comfort. The children were forgotten by everyone. There was no intention to leave the children to cope with it on their own; everybody was just lost in the overwhelming grief that engulfed their parents.

In May 1992, seven months after the murder, the trial got under way in the Four Courts. Ciaran had gone to the first court appearance of Michael Dean McLoughlin, the man charged with murdering his daughter, expecting to see a vision of evil. What he saw was a really good-looking young man, smartly dressed and well groomed. He could have been anybody's brother or son; nothing about him said 'murderer'.

The Gardaí had arrived at McLoughlin's door shortly after the murder. At 3.45pm on 1 November, Jill's uncle Declan Bishop pointed him out to a local garda as the man last seen with Jill. The following day McLoughlin made a statement in Bray Garda Station admitting that he had met Jill, but claiming that he had walked away after a scuffle outside the disco.

Despite his attempt to lie about events that night, forensic evidence uncovered the truth. A piece of human flesh found on McLoughlin's jacket matched Jill's blood type. Her blood also matched a bloodstain found on the sole of McLoughlin's boot. In a second statement taken by Serious Crime Squad detectives, McLoughlin admitted the killing.

The court was told in evidence that McLoughlin had fallen out with his girlfriend that night. During the trial McLoughlin admitted he had killed Jill, but claimed that he only lashed out after she called him a 'queer'. It was a blatant bid for a manslaughter verdict, an insinuation that Jill was in some way responsible for the violence he unleashed on her. There was no-one to give Jill's side of the story.

For the Bishops, McLoughlin's efforts to avoid a murder conviction by pleading not guilty meant five gruelling days in court. Some days they arrived and there was nowhere for them to sit in the packed courtroom. Ciaran already knew that some of the seats in the public gallery during high-profile cases were routinely taken up by court-watchers – people with no involvement in the trial, but who brought packed lunches to the courtroom and hung on every detail of the trial like it was live soap opera.

'I had no intention of raping her. I was never a violent man. I just lost the head,' McLoughlin told the jury. He claimed he put the coin in her mouth after she had stopped screaming. The post-mortem evidence told a different and much more disturbing story about the savagery of his assault.

On 15 May 1992, the jury of six men and six women took just over two hours to come to a verdict in the case. 'You have been found guilty of murder,' Judge Paul Carney told McLoughlin. 'I sentence you to imprisonment for life.'

The fact that McLoughlin was convicted of murder was a tremendous relief to the Bishops. Anything less would have been a slight against Jill. An initial murder charge can often result in a lesser conviction for manslaughter.

If it had been a manslaughter verdict, that would have meant for Ciaran and May that Jill was in some way implicated in her own death. As it was, her innocence remained intact. That was why her murder affected so many people, Ciaran believes.

'She was a good kid. There was no baggage coming anywhere. She was an innocent kid. She was everybody's child – that's why people were affected by it. She wasn't taking drugs, she wasn't drinking – maybe she was taking the odd one – she was your average little kid just going about life innocently and somebody just took her away. I think that hit everybody, and then there was the cruelty of it.'

As far as the Bishops are concerned, the State did nothing for them in the aftermath of Jill's murder. The Criminal Injuries Compensation Board paid out the standard £17,000 award to the family of a murder victim. But £2,000 of that was paid to the solicitor who made the application for the payment.

There was no financial support for medical bills of family members who have had to have ongoing treatment. Once the wheels of the criminal justice system had turned, the family were expected to pick themselves up, walk away and get on with their lives.

After the trial, Ciaran Bishop was still searching for help. The first person to talk in a way that reached him was psychologist John Donohue, who gave a lecture at the Ilac Centre in Dublin city centre on traumatic bereavement. Ciaran spoke to him after the lecture and the two men became friends.

One night they met for pints in the Yellow House pub in Rathfarnham. Over the drinks they discussed how desperately the families of murder victims needed a support system. John kept telling Ciaran that it had to be set up by someone who had been through it themselves. 'Yes, absolutely,' Ciaran agreed. 'But who could we get to do it?'

Eventually John told him that Ciaran himself would have to spearhead it. In 1993 Ciaran approached Victim Support with the idea for The Jill Project. He wanted it to be a memoriam to Jill. In the end it was called the Families of Murder Victims.

The two men interviewed people to work as counsellors, or listeners as Ciaran preferred to call them. During some of the interviews he was disturbed that some of the candidates appeared to have a weird fascination with murder rather than a desire to help and support families.

In the end it was Ciaran himself who did a lot of the listening. A helpline was set up on the Bishops' home phone line, and sometimes Ciaran would find himself talking to a relative of a murder victim late into the night. On other occasions the Gardaí asked him to visit someone they felt needed counselling in the aftermath of a murder. 'Murder' is a word that he insists is the only way to describe what happened. He hates it when people refer to 'the tragedy'.

That first Christmas, less than two months after Jill's death, was a quiet one in the Bishop house. Their usual Christmas visitors stayed away, even though the drinks cabinet had been stocked as usual in an effort to get through it as normal. Twelve years on, Christmas is still the most difficult time of the year. The anniversary of Jill's murder is also very painful. On the twelfth anniversary of her death, Ciaran found himself going to bed at five o'clock in the afternoon and sleeping through until the next day, not wanting to be awake for the anniversary hours.

Nonetheless, Christmas 2001 brought a real boost when two bits of good luck came their way. At Leopardstown on Stephen's Day, Ciaran backed Florida Pearl in an English race and won at eight to one. The next morning a member of his Lotto syndicate phoned to say they had won the Lotto.

There were three winning tickets and the forty members of the Credit Union syndicate had won £600,000, a third of the jackpot. Then, in a dramatic twist, the Bank of Ireland in Baggot Street lost the winning ticket. In the commotion around the euro changeover, a bank official had mistakenly put the envelope which had been handed into the bank in a mail bag. Two weeks later it turned up and was posted back to syndicate members, but not before the bank was publicly embarrassed into paying out the money. Each member got around £21,000.

Other joys have been the Bishops' grandchildren. Their son John's children, Corey and Chloe, have brought a new happiness. May minds her granddaughter and the child is as loving and affectionate as her aunt Jill was. On Sunday mornings they wonder what the neighbours make of the sing-songs orchestrated by Chloe of her favourite nursery rhymes.

In the background there is a clock ticking. Twelve years after he was jailed for life, Michael Dean McLoughlin is likely to be released at some time in the near future.

In 2001 Ciaran got a phone call from his parish priest asking him to come down for a chat. When he arrived the priest told him it was about Dean McLoughlin. He had received a call from the prison chaplain who wanted him to relay the news to the Bishops that Dean was really sorry about what happened to Jill. The message through the priests was that Dean wanted them to know their daughter was a very nice person, and he could not understand why he had killed her.

Ciaran was furious. He was delighted that the governor was pleased with McLoughlin's progress and that he was looking so well, he told the priest bitterly. He was delighted that the chaplain was so concerned about him and he was delighted that the prison governor was worrying about him. But who, he asked the priest, was worrying about the Bishop family, and helping to prepare them for McLoughlin's release?

Asked if he had any message to relay back to his daughter's murderer, Ciaran said there was absolutely nothing he wanted to say to him.

Under the terms of a life sentence, Michael Dean McLoughlin's future will be decided by the Minister for Justice of the day, who must approve or reject any recommendation from the Parole Board. The average sentence served by a lifer is twelve years to fourteen years. It is likely that McLoughlin will still be in his thirties when he is released from prison. The Bishops have to face the 'doomsday' scenario that he will still be a young man when he is released, with his life ahead of him.

Every week they put fresh flowers on Jill's grave. She is buried with her grandparents.

It is not for him to forgive his daughter's killer, Ciaran believes. Forgiveness would be some kind of acceptance that his daughter only wanted to live for eighteen years, that she wanted to be hurt and left for dead. Jill is the only one who can forgive.

'I listen to the radio in the morning and sometimes when I hear there's been a suicide in Mountjoy or any prison I listen very intently. And then I hear a name and when it's not his I'm kind of disappointed. He really has destroyed us. But I feel we've beaten him as well. We're still together, still intact and still fighting the battle.'

Chapter 3

That's not my son you're talking about

Marian Edwards is waiting to get the hat back. She does not know how it will affect her when she has it in her hands. The smell of her son's hair will probably have faded from its fibres. But the blood stains will still be there. The gardaí have warned her that the hat her son wore that morning in August 2001 still has his blood on it. But she wants it back. It was Jonathan's and she wants it back.

She saw the hat lying on the ground in St Mary's Park in Limerick when she rushed there that morning after hearing that her son had been injured. She saw the hat on the ground, along with a quilt hastily grabbed from someone's bed. But her aunt pulled her back from running over to pick them up. Jonathan Edwards had gone in the ambulance and her husband was in the car behind, she was told.

Sometime after she rushed to the casualty department at Limerick Regional Hospital, the hat was placed in a Garda evidence bag. Twenty-six months after Jonathan's death, Marian went down to the Garda station asking about the hat. They have promised to give it to her.

In less than twelve hours on the night of Monday, 27 August 2001, through to the Tuesday morning, two young Limerick men were killed. One of the deaths would become a notorious case two years later in November 2003, as political pressure to deal with crime in Limerick piled onto the Minister for Justice after the collapse of the murder trial. The other death and subsequent murder trial would have terrible repercussions for the Edwards family.

Eric Leamy and Jonathan Edwards died within hours of each other. Jonathan's killing has been described in court as a revenge attack for the death of eighteen-year-old Eric after a fight in the Edwards' former home estate of St Mary's Park. The two deaths sparked talk of gang warfare in Limerick. Rows in schoolyards led to shootings and stabbings, as the city was torn apart by a small number of feuding families living on top of one another in Limerick's poor housing estates.

Sixteen years before that August morning, Marian Edwards made a decision to leave St Mary's Park to try and change the course of her children's lives. She had married her husband Patrick at the age of seventeen and they now had four small children. St Mary's Park was her childhood home. It was also where her parents had grown up and where, if she stayed, her own children would grow up.

She decided to leave the estate and move to Corbally on the outskirts of the city. It was a short distance away, but with fewer problems, and Marian felt her kids would have a better chance there. She worked hard to keep the family going. By the time Jonathan died she had three jobs. She worked as a cleaner – tough, physical work. But she had a great circle of work friends. Her big treat was not a night at the pub, but a trip to town, a look around the shops and a coffee and a chat with friends.

Marian lost her first baby – a boy who died just eight days after he was born. Then her eldest daughter Nicola was born.

Next came Jonathan, on 5 September 1979, and then two more boys, Bryan and Garrett. The family was living in Corbally in 1991 when Stewart, their youngest boy, was born.

When he finished primary school in 1993, Jonathan was one of a number of unlucky children. One hundred and sixty Limerick boys, most of them from working-class estates around the city, were left without a secondary school place, exposing the dire need for more secondary school facilities in Limerick. One hundred of the boys were taken on by one secondary school, leaving sixty young boys with no place. The issue was raised in the Dáil and the government was called on to act in response to this shocking neglect of education in the city.

After parents like Marian and Patrick marched to demand a new secondary school, the Christian Brothers established their first new school in a quarter of a century. The Edmund Rice College opened in the vacant wing of a local national school.

Jonathan was among the boys who finally started his secondary education in the new school on the Shelbourne Road. But by then he had lost interest. He stayed on until second year and then started to mitch class. Still only in his early teens, he felt he was a dropout and that school had nothing to offer him. His parents decided it would be better to let him leave school and find his feet, rather than to keep up the pretence that he was going there every day.

He spent some time attending the local youth centre and then Marian found him some cleaning jobs with her agency. She says he was a good little worker. He went on to work at the abattoir on the Dock Road until he learned to drive. After that he got some driving work with Golden Vale. He was working in the Curtronics plant in Shannon when his relationship with his girlfriend broke down.

Jonathan had a baby girl, Chloe, with his girlfriend, and she was pregnant with his second daughter when they decided to end the relationship. Jonathan left his job and moved back home to Corbally.

By the time he died his new girlfriend Lisa was eight weeks pregnant with his third child – a son. The boy is called Jonathan. His smiling photograph sits at one end of his grandmother's mantelpiece; her own boy's smiling face sits at the other.

Marian sees her grandson, but some days she is not able to see him. There are the black days. There are the crying days and there are the days when she cannot bear to be around anyone.

Her grandson sleeps in his father's old bed. Marian cried for hours as she dismantled the bed where her son had slept to give it to his girlfriend for the baby.

'His children won't give me back him,' Marian says. 'I can be their grandmother. I can never be their mother.'

For Jonathan's parents the only available account of what happened on that night in August 2001 jars horribly with their memory of the young man they knew and loved.

Their son's nickname was Taz. It had been the name of his favourite dog, a Staffordshire bull terrier. Jonathan bred dogs and kept them, along with his pigeons, in the back garden of the Edwards house at Corbally. Taz was such a beloved pet that when the dog died Jonathan got a terrier's head tattooed on his left shoulder, with the name Taz in ink underneath. It became his own nickname.

His father remembers Jonathan staying up at night if one of his dogs was sick. As a boy he was animal-mad and the dog-breeding and pigeon fraternity provided a wide circle of friends. His school and his work took second place to the dogs and pigeons.

He had been in trouble with the Gardaí once, being arrested with a small amount of cannabis on him. His parents got him a solicitor and stood by him. He was fined £120 and the garda who had arrested him on the drug offence spoke highly of Jonathan at his murder trial.

His unemployment assistance payments were usually spent the same way every week: some money to his girlfriend for child support, food for the dogs and pigeons and a bit of money for himself. His mother believes money was never an issue for him. If he had it he spent it. If he was broke he wasn't worried.

It is a matter of deep hurt for Marian that the story of what happened in St Mary's Park in August 2001 revolves around a dog – a German shepherd pup – and Jonathan's treatment of it.

She knows some of the facts of what happened in the run-up to his death. Most of what she has, however, is merely the version given at the subsequent trial, a version that does not square with her knowledge of her son's character.

Jonathan had bought the pup from a boy in St Mary's Park and had brought it to his girlfriend's cousin's house. The dog was limping that Monday morning, and Jonathan asked Marian later that day for £20 to take it to the vet. His mother saw he had been drinking. Afraid that the money might just go on more drink she said she would not give him the £20 then, but would leave it for him in the house the next morning.

Marian's worries were elsewhere that day. Her daughter Nicola was thirty weeks pregnant and they had just found out that the baby had a heart defect. Jonathan was getting ready to go out that evening when he came into the living room.

'Well, sis, did you get any news from Dublin?' he asked Nicola.
'I'm going up on Friday, Jonathan.'

'Don't worry,' said Jonathan. 'I'll be going up with Mam and if we've to stay in the car park you'll be all right.' He went out the door calling back to Marian, 'Mam, I'll see you in the morning.'

He was going to cycle into the city, but Marian asked Paul Maguire, an old neighbour, to give him a lift as far as St Mary's Park. That act would be one of the 'ifs' about Jonathan's death that now haunt her. There is always the question, what might have happened if she hadn't asked Paul to give him a lift?

At around 10.15 that evening, her sister Rosa rang her from the estate to say that Jonathan was out with the German shepherd pup and he seemed to have been drinking. Marian told her to take no notice of him. Rosa told Marian that Jonathan was talking to the dog. 'That's nothing new, Rosa. He talks to the dog the whole time,' Marian told her.

At 8.40 the next morning she rang Rachel Quinliven, Jonathan's girlfriend's cousin whom he often stayed with. Rachel told Marian he was in bed asleep. Marian told her to tell him the £20 for the vet was under the microwave at home, and his clean clothes were in the house.

Twenty-six months after he died, that is all Marian Edwards knows for sure about the last hours of her son's life. Later at the trial, evidence would be given that Eric Leamy's death was a result of a fight over Jonathan's treatment of the pup.

Jonathan met a group of young men and, so the evidence went, kicked the dog. The men objected to this and Jonathan left the pup there and went away. Later he returned with another man, the court was told. And in the ensuing row Eric Leamy was stabbed to death.

Nothing about this story makes sense to Jonathan's parents. They can never see him being cruel to an animal, especially not a dog.

Marian says she is not the kind of mother who could defend her son if he had been in any way responsible for Eric Leamy's death. Gardaí have told her that he was in the vicinity, like more than a dozen other young men that night, but he was not the man who attacked the teenager.

The next morning tension on the estate was high. Marian knew nothing of the stabbing and was at the maternity unit of Limerick Hospital with Nicola. Her mobile phone rang. It was Nicola's boyfriend's mother, with news that Jonathan had had an argument in St Mary's Park.

When Marian got to St Ita's Road in the estate, her aunt held her back. She saw Jonathan's hat, and a quilt that someone had put over him before the ambulance arrived, lying on the pavement. She rushed to follow the ambulance to the hospital.

Both Eric Leamy and Jonathan Edwards had arrived at the same casualty unit in the space of those few hours. Marian recognised sixteen-year-old Willie Moran, a youth she knew from St Mary's Park, at the hospital with another young man.

At 11.30 Lisa, Jonathan's girlfriend, arrived at the hospital and told Marian that it had been Willie Moran who had hit Jonathan. As the clock ticked and Jonathan's condition did not improve, the doctors decided to transfer him to Cork Hospital.

In Cork, Marian got the first sight of her son since the night before when he had said goodbye. She knew by looking at him that he would not be coming home. There was no coming back from where he was.

The post mortem would eventually show that Jonathan had died from a single blow delivered with force from a height down on his head. A fragment of skull bone was driven into his brain. From her understanding of the post mortem, Marian believes that her son was dead when he hit the ground.

He never regained consciousness. He never got to tell his side of the story of the German shepherd pup, the stabbing of Eric Leamy and the minutes before his own death.

The day of Jonathan's twenty-first birthday, the September before, had been something of a relief for Marian. After his teenage friend Luke McEvoy had been killed in a car accident some years earlier, Jonathan had always told his mother he would not live to be old. 'You'll be lucky if I see twenty-one,' he would say to her. He went out for dinner the night of his twenty-first with his girlfriend. Little did she know he would buried on the day of his twenty-second birthday.

Luke's death had left Jonathan with another idea. Along with gaining his fear that he would die young, he now told his mother that he wanted to donate his organs. 'Mam, if any-thing happens, give what you can, but don't give my eyes,' he told her.

At Cork Hospital Nicola asked the doctors about Jonathan's blood type. It emerged that he had a rare type. As a healthy young man who had suffered a brain injury, his organs were perfect for harvesting. Marian informed the doctors and on Friday, 31 August, she had to make the hardest decision of her life – to switch off the life-support machine. His healthy heart continued to pump for hours before he finally stopped breathing.

They found a donor card among his belongings months after his death. He had indicated on the signed card that all his organs apart from his eyes should be given.

In the run-up to Christmas 2002, Marian received a beautiful Christmas card from the two men who received Jonathan's organs. One of them, a young father like Jonathan, had been on dialysis for years and his future looked bleak. The unit at Beaumont where the transplants were organised have sent her a certificate from the roll of honour where Jonathan's name has been added as an organ donor. It is framed on the sitting room wall alongside photographs of him. They offered Marian a chance to meet the two men whose lives have been saved by her son's death. She does not think it is something she can do. It is too painful an idea. She would be looking for something of Jonathan in them.

Jonathan's sister Nicola tried to make sense of her brother's death in the days afterwards by saying that he would make sure her baby would be okay. His promise to her that he would sleep in the car park to make sure was the last thing he had said to her. 'Jonathan will look after me,' she would say to Marian. 'He'll make everything all right.'

But that was not to be. A month after the night and morning of violence in St Mary's Park, Nicola's daughter, Casey, was born. She died the next day. Marian had buried her son on 5 September and left for Dublin where Nicola was in hospital four days later. She did not return with Nicola for five weeks, a terrible journey home without a baby.

Marian spent eight months swamped by her own grief before she realised her husband had lost his son and her children their brother.

'My son's death was my biggest loss and I couldn't talk to my children about Jonathan. I really couldn't let them know how I felt. It would be like I was putting more pain on them than they were able for.'

Bryan and Jonathan had shared a room. When his dog had pups, Jonathan had given Garrett one. The relationship was one of hero worship from the younger brothers to their older sibling. Bryan sobbed himself to sleep for months after Jonathan's death. He still cries uncontrollably and Marian is hoping he will speak to a counsellor. Garrett, who was closest in age to Jonathan, shows less emotion. As the eldest boy he feels that he must be strong for the whole family.

At Jonathan's funeral his popularity with the girls was brought home to his mother as she saw young women, some of whom had left the city after finishing school, arrive at the church to pay their respects. At his 'month's mind' Mass the priest remarked that he had never seen a church so full after the death of a young person.

In the months that followed, Marian began to think she was losing her mind. Clattering around her head were the ifs, buts and whys of Jonathan's death. She started to go to Victim Support meetings to try and talk about what she was feeling.

Then there was a stage, ten months after Jonathan's death, that she was gripped with an intense physical longing to hold him. 'I wanted to hold him. I had this thing of if I could hold him, if he could tell me did he call out for me that morning … To some people they're stupid things but to someone that has lost a child they're things that go on in your head. The first time it rained I got very emotional because he was up there in the graveyard on his own and to me, in my head, he was going to be drowned.'

Even though her son was a grown man and a father of three children, she desperately worried that her child was on his own with no-one to mind him when they left him behind in the graveyard after the funeral.

Willie Moran Junior was first arrested and charged with assault causing serious harm and then, after Jonathan's death, he was charged with murder. In November 2002 his father Willie Moran Senior was also charged with Jonathan's murder. At a bail hearing in January 2003 the court was told that the older man was facing a murder charge because he stopped Jonathan from escaping from the attack.

Willie Moran Senior never stood trial for Jonathan's murder. The DPP withdrew the charges after the outcome of the trial of his teenage son.

Marian refused to talk to reporters about Jonathan. She brought a photograph into the offices of a local newspaper to have an anniversary and birthday notice put in. When she bought the paper she saw the photograph reproduced on the news pages as a picture of the murder victim who had been in the news.

There was an eighteen-month wait for the trial to start. Marian asked the gardaí why the father and son accused of the murder were not being tried together. She was told that it had been decided that there were to be separate trials and there could be no mention during his son's trial of Willie Moran Senior and the fact that he was also facing a murder charge.

It began in the Central Criminal Court, sitting in the Four Courts in Dublin, on Monday, 31 March 2003. There were three days of hearings that week and then three days the following week. Some of the time, when the defence team cross-examined witnesses, Marian had to stop herself jumping up and shouting the words that were screaming around in her head. 'That's not my son you're talking about,' she wanted to shout as the defence team built a picture of a menacing bully who was killed in an act of self-defence.

Jonathan Edwards was five-foot-eight and of a slight build, Marian says. She felt like standing up and showing the jury a picture of him. On Tuesday, 8 April, Marian told her daughter Nicola that she believed the teenager accused of her son's murder would not be found guilty. The following day, after deliberating for five hours, the jury acquitted nineteen-year-old Willie Moran Junior after they accepted the defence argument that he had acted in self-defence. As they walked out of the Four Courts, devastated by the verdict, Nicola remarked to her mother, 'I feel like they just killed my brother all over again.'

It is one of the nightmares families face as a murder trial looms. The accused person has a legal right to a presumption of innocence and their legal team has an obligation to fight to prove that innocence. In many cases where a murder charge is fought rather than a guilty plea being entered, the families of murder victims feel it is the character of the dead victim that is on trial. The more a good defence barrister can detract from the reputation of the victim the better it will serve their client in the eyes of the jury.

In their Manifesto of Rights for those bereaved by murder, Victim Support have identified one single issue that stands above all others as a right that is not being met for the families of murder victims: the 'consistent provision of clear and accurate information' about the murder case is vital to reduce the feeling that families are ignored and left out of the investigative and judicial processes.

Nothing will prepare a family to hear their loved one's character kicked around a courtroom, but information about the rules of engagement during a criminal trial is important to help families to understand why it feels like their loved one is on trial.

Marian does not know how she would feel if the verdict had gone the other way. 'If they had given them life I don't know, because I'm doing a life sentence – my life will never be the same. I'm forty-five. I've no motivation. There's part of me gone that I can never replace and what's left is the loneliness and the want for him.'

After twenty years off the cigarettes she is now smoking again. Her busy social and working life has shrunk back in on itself. She rarely goes out. The Victim Support meetings were too difficult to return to after the trial. She did not want to see other families who were facing the prospect of a murder trial knowing how it felt to see someone acquitted at the expense of her dead son's reputation.

What happened in Jonathan Edwards' case is very much the exception to the rule. Acquittals in murder trials are uncommon. A far more common outcome is for someone charged with murder to be found guilty of a lesser charge – manslaughter or serious assault. For some families a manslaughter verdict can seem almost as bad as an acquittal. In the eyes of the family, a manslaughter verdict is an insinuation that the victim was in some way to blame for their own death.

Nonetheless a manslaughter verdict does not generally result in the defendant walking free from the Four Courts and, as in the Edwards case, back to the streets of the city where the family of the dead man lives.

The latest available figures from the Courts Service on the number of murder trials in the country show that an average of one murder case a week came to the Central Criminal Court in 2002.

Fifty-five murder cases were sent for trial in 2002, of which forty-eight were dealt with. Of those forty-eight cases, thirty-eight resulted in a conviction. Just over half of all convictions were on lesser charges than murder. Twenty of those thirty-eight convictions were for manslaughter and other charges.

In 2002 there were eighteen murder convictions out of the total of fifty-five murder cases that went to trial. More than half of the fifty-five cases – twenty-eight cases – went to a full trial with the defendant pleading not guilty.

Of the twenty-eight murder cases heard where the defendant pleaded not guilty, sixteen cases, or just over half of them, resulted in a murder conviction.

In a further eleven of the twenty-eight full murder trials, the defendant was convicted of manslaughter or other offences. In the twenty-eighth case the jury failed to reach agreement. In a case like this, a retrial is a possibility in the future.

In 2001 there had been just three murder acquittals in the Central Criminal Court. There were no acquittals in 2002.

In November 2003 another Limerick mother watched a man accused of her son's murder walk free. 'The likes of what has happened in this case has never been encountered in this court before,' Justice Paul Carney said as he dismissed the jury after the collapse of the trial of Liam Keane, who had been accused of the murder of Eric Leamy that night in August 2001.

Nineteen-year-old Liam Keane walked free after crucial prosecution witnesses changed their evidence or retracted their statements. Judge Carney had remarked that the witnesses seemed to be suffering from 'collective amnesia' about the events that night in St Mary's Park.

The day after the collapse of the trial the daily newspapers showed large photographs of Liam Keane victorious and free. The Dáil erupted and Justice Minister Michael McDowell responded by finding an extra 02 million in the Department of Justice budget for Garda operations against crime gangs. McDowell said he would also consider changing the laws of evidence in criminal trials.

Had he been alive, Jonathan Edwards would probably have been a witness at the trial. As it was, the events in the Central Criminal Court brought back all the details of his death and once again the Limerick murder was headline news.

After the Keane trial there were now two men accused of the murders of two young men back on the streets. 'If my son had died of an illness or was killed by a car I would have accepted it,' Marian says. 'But to be taken by the hands of others – that's something else. They've left three orphans. He had three brothers and a sister, a mother and a father. He had grandparents and aunts. They didn't just destroy my son that morning. They destroyed a whole family.'

She is left with a lump of bitterness lodged in her chest. The bitterness is not something she wants or embraces. It saps her. She pushes herself to get out of bed, to get dressed, to be a mother to her young son and give him a normal childhood. There is also fear for her other children, that there will be another knock on the door with terrible news. There is the fear that her two older sons' anger will lead them to do something they and she would regret forever.

She could move away, leave Limerick and all its feuds and claustrophobic hatreds, but the wrench from the house would be too much. Her memories are there. Jonathan is there, in every corner of the house. When she looks out her kitchen window in the morning she sees him in the back garden, where he spent most of his days. That's where his friends waked him when they came to pay their respects, with a few cans in the back garden after he was laid out in the house on his twenty-second birthday.

The armchair nearest the window in the front room is where he would sit, with his feet on the windowsill, waiting and watching for friends coming up towards the house. The front wall is where he sat and charmed and flirted with the girls coming home from school.

Jonathan grins down from the mantelpiece. His teeth were his glory, she remembers. She spent a small fortune over the years on toothpaste and new toothbrushes.

Marian Edwards worked to get a life for her family away from St Mary's Park. When her children were grown up there was only so far away from the estate that she could keep them as they moved in their own social circles. Despite all her efforts, Jonathan Edwards' presence there that night in August 2001 sealed his fate. 'To me he was in the wrong place at the wrong time,' says Marian, 'and he suffered as a result of that.'

Chapter 4

The worst nightmare
to come to anyone's door

He came to Dolores wrapped in a blanket. He was just a tiny, warm body with pink cheeks. She wanted to say goodbye the same way. 'Please just wrap him in a towel and let me hold him. I'm not afraid. It's me own child. I know it's only bones, but I'm not afraid,' she begged gardaí.

Patrick Lawlor was seventeen when he was killed and buried three feet underground, near a trench at the ninth lock of the Grand Canal in Clondalkin, west Dublin. He was found in January 2002, three years and nineteen days after his mother, Dolores Lawlor, last saw him alive.

In the end she did not get to hold what was left of her son, but instead said her goodbye by resting her head back against the wall of a vault housing his body, while the detective who led the search for him said a decade of the rosary with her. She never got the physical closeness that she longed for. She had to explain to her children that all that was left of him were skeletal remains, kept frozen in the vault for thirteen weeks until the paperwork and the DNA testing were completed and he could be buried in the cemetery plot she had bought for him while he was still missing.

Dolores went to forty-two weeks when she was pregnant with Patrick. As the baby was late, she was brought into hospital. There were six others on the ward, and she remembers that he was the only baby that survived.

He was purple when he was born and she saw the doctors running off with him. She was wheeled outside the delivery room and left on a trolley. Patrick was her fourth child. The babies had come in quick succession and the matron in the maternity unit knew Dolores. She asked her why she was crying. 'They've taken my baby,' Dolores told her. 'There must be something wrong with him, because I'm lying here ages.'

The matron brought him back. 'He was wrapped in a little blanket, his cheeks were really pink,' Dolores recalls. He was placed in her arms and Dolores went off to sleep on the trolley.

Patrick survived a difficult birth, and that longing to hold him stayed with Dolores for the three years that he was missing. She still longs to hold him.

From his six-pound weight, Patrick grew into a big, jolly baby. She remembers him sitting in his pram with a bit of bread and a cheeky grin. At eight-and-a-half months he was crawling. Two weeks later he stood on his little legs and walked.

Dolores is something of a legend in Ballyfermot. Dolores Plunkett – she is known by her maiden name – and her big bus. It was not a real bus, but a crocodile of kids led by a big old Silver Cross pram. There was usually a baby in the pram, another underneath and six or seven kids walking along behind.

She came from a big Ballyfermot family herself, with six brothers and three sisters, so her ten children – seven boys and three girls – repeated the pattern.

Her neighbours used to ask her to move Patrick's cot away from the wall. He would pull himself up on his hunkers and rock the cot, banging it against the wall for hours. Her postman remembers him as the little lad who would greet him at the door saying, 'Postman Pat, will you tie my laces?' The boy would be standing in the doorway with his shoes on the wrong feet.

Dolores' small Corporation house was never quiet. At Christmas the kids threw themselves into the season with gusto. Two pals came in one Christmas Eve to see the scene, the fire blazing and all the kids washed and in their pyjamas. 'This house is real Christmassy,' the friend said. 'But where do you put them all, Dolores?' She showed them the bedrooms with bunk beds crammed in. 'They were saying, "Jaysus, it was like Snow White and the Seven Dwarves, only I had ten."'

Dolores' marriage broke up around the time that Patrick was making his First Communion. Coming home one day, he burst into tears. When she asked what was wrong he said everyone needed to have a daddy to make their communion and he had no daddy.

He took the break-up hard. As Dolores' shadow, he was the first in the firing line when she was angry about something. He watched his parents' marriage disintegrate and took it all to heart. After her children's father moved out Dolores got on with the business of rearing her brood.

Her eldest son, John, took Patrick to Croke Park one day after his school got into the schoolboy finals. Standing up in the back bedroom she watched them walking across the grass towards the house. Even in the distance, she could tell from the slope of the two boys' shoulders and their weary trudge that things had not gone well.

When he got inside, John refused even to take the runner-up medals out of his bag. 'He's not coming with me any more,' he said angrily pointing at Patrick. The younger boy started to laugh. It turned out that one of the rival supporters had started teasing them about Ballyfermot and Patrick squared up to him, even though he was almost twice his size. The row got him barred from Croke Park.

She remembers her son as a good kid, always by her side. Patrick suffered from asthma as a child, as did his brother Stephen. One night Dolores got so worried about Stephen's asthma that she sent Patrick out to run round to her mother's and call an ambulance. There was no phone in their house. It was lashing rain outside and Patrick ended up on the nebuliser in the bed beside his brother in Our Lady's Hospital after the late-night dash brought on his own asthma attack.

By the age of sixteen Patrick had become a father. His daughter Shanice was nine months old when he died.

It was the Autumn of 1998 when Dolores' world started to crumble. She got a phone call to come down to Ballyfermot Garda Station, where Patrick was being held in a cell. He had been arrested in a house near his home in Gallanstown with a stash of drugs and money. It was the first Dolores knew that Patrick had anything to do with drugs, and it was news to her that he was using heroin.

She remembered he had recently been very sick and she spent days with him in the sitting room rubbing his back and looking after him as if he was a small child again. She used to rub a pattern on his back as a baby when he had difficulty breathing, to soothe and calm him. Whenever he was sick she returned to the old routine, rubbing his back, comforting her son.

She thought he had a lung infection that time, he was so sick. At times over those few days in the living room he was bathed in sweat. It was only later that his girlfriend told Dolores that her son had been going through withdrawal from heroin.

After the arrest Dolores brought him to Fortune House, a drug counselling service in the area, and he went to a few sessions. Her GP offered to take him on a private methadone programme, but Patrick was not willing.

Then Dolores made a decision that still stops her in her tracks when she talks about it. It leaves her struggling to breathe when she thinks about what she was forced to do. Like many parents, she could not risk her other children's futures by allowing a heroin-addicted child to stay living in the house. It broke her heart, but she had to put him out.

She still wonders if she could have done more to help Patrick, without dragging the rest of the family down. 'It's terrible when the world's against you, and he had no-one. I feel he had nobody. Drugs are a curse, the worst nightmare to come to anyone's door.'

Patrick moved out of the house to a flat in Palmerstown, but would still come home to her almost every day for a meal.

On Wednesday, 6 January 1999, Patrick called to Gallanstown for his usual visit with his mother. She was standing in the window when he walked up the path and for a minute she did not recognise him. He had his back to her and she thought he had lost a lot of weight. He came in and asked a favour. 'Mam, can I have a bath, because the shower's broke in the flat.'

She had to go out, and when she left he was asleep in a chair. At 4.20 that day she came back. She urged him to go before the other kids came home and there was a row about him being there. 'Patrick, come on, son, you have to go.'

Dolores had her grandson James with her and was bending down to see to the toddler when Patrick walked out into the hall. She just looked up at him and he said, 'Goodbye, Mam.'

It was only later it struck her that there was something wrong. Her son never usually said 'goodbye,' just 'see ya later,' or 'see you, mam.'

That Friday she went to Laytown for a friend's birthday party. The next morning Patrick was due to go swimming with a family friend, but never turned up. For the next fortnight Dolores went looking for her son – calling to his friends, going to hostels for the homeless and to hospitals and visiting the flat on Manor Road in Palmerstown where he had been staying.

On 20 January she reported him missing at Ballyfermot Garda Station. They issued the standard description carried in newspapers the next day. 'He is 5ft 8ins, about 10st, with blue eyes, fair complexion and short, brown hair. Anyone with information is asked to contact Ballyfermot Garda Station,' the report read.

Gardaí searched the flat after she had gone to get Patrick's clothes. Her ex-husband then told her through someone else that four men had come looking for him to tell him that Patrick had been in an accident.

The passing of two landmark dates convinced Dolores that her son was dead – her own birthday at the end of March and Patrick's daughter's first birthday in April 1999. That, and the fact that there was no sign of him looking for his asthma medication, was confirmation that the worst had happened.

Dolores realised that a young man going missing would not top anyone's priority list, and she set about tracing the family who had lived in the house where the drugs were seized. She got a phone number in England and made contact. Then she went down to the Garda station to demand to know why they could not have done the same.

She came out of the station in tears and said to herself. 'Now, Dolores, it's up to you.' So she started the first poster campaign.

She used to get upset when people did not believe her when she told them her son had been murdered. Some suggested he might be in hiding. But she knew that he needed support to survive. As far as she was concerned, even if he was involved in the world of drugs, he was no crime lord with the comfort zone of houses and cars. 'The child had nothing. How he survived out there I'll never know.'

Despite the trauma of Patrick's disappearance family life had to take on the appearance of being normal. Dolores' youngest boy, Tommy, was only seven when Patrick went missing. 'It was like living two separate lives: one normal and the other in the world of the unknown.' It was at night, in the quiet of her bed, that Dolores tried to think up new ways of keeping the search going.

Detective Sergeant Padraig Kennedy was assigned to the case and he came to introduce himself and his colleague, Superintendent Eddie Finucane, to Dolores. He urged her to redo the poster. She insisted that this time it should feature a picture of herself with Patrick. Even though she was well-known in the area, many people who knew her did not realise that the missing boy was her son.

The picture of the two of them was taken at her fortieth birthday, the last birthday he had shared with her. The posters went up and her efforts continued.

By September 2002 it had been over two-and-a-half years since she had last seen Patrick and there was still no trace of him. She phoned a group in Kilkenny who were putting together a sculpture to commemorate Ireland's missing people. The monument, by sculptor Ann Mulrooney, was made up of casts of palm prints of the relatives of missing people. The sculpture was erected in the grounds of Kilkenny Castle, the home county of the missing young woman JoJo Dullard, whose sister Mary Phelan was behind the venture.

Unfortunately, it was too late for Dolores' palm print to be included. So she set about creating her own memorial. Her parish priest in Ballyfermot agreed that a spot could be found in a new peace garden he was creating in the grounds of the church.

When they unwrapped the small granite memorial slab with Patrick's photograph set into it, she could have sworn her son's face had changed since the last time she saw the picture. 'That kid is smiling at me,' she thought to herself. 'There's something up.'

'A loving son, brother, father and grandson. Missing since 6th January 1999, aged 17 years. Always in our thoughts. Pray for him,' the plaque on the wall of the new garden reads. At the unveiling ceremony, Detective Sergeant Kennedy promised Dolores that she would have a headstone, that this garden on the side of a busy road would not be the only place where she could go to visit her son.

The search for Patrick continued, with regular expeditions by the gardaí to try and find him. A body in a shallow grave leaves its own sign. Over time the earth packed around the corpse sinks, leaving a tell-tale depression in the surface of the soil. Because it has been dug up, the earth is packed more loosely when it is put back over a body and an implement like a pole or a shovel can be pushed right down into it, unlike an area that has never been dug.

In September 1999, gardaí at Ballyfermot Garda Station received an anonymous telephone call with a tip-off about the whereabouts of Patrick's body. An appeal was broadcast on the RTÉ 'Crimeline' programme for the caller to get back in touch.

Areas of land at the back of an ESB power station and the Semperit tyre factory in west Dublin were searched. The garda dog unit had just taken delivery of a specially-trained cadaver dog. The German shepherd was a sniffer dog trained to hunt for the smell of human remains through aeration pipes put into the suspected site of a shallow grave. Despite prolonged efforts and the new search methods, nothing was found. Until they had a precise location based on more than rumour and anonymous phone calls, there was unlikely to be a breakthrough.

In January 2002 Gary Clarke, a Ballyfermot heroin addict, was arrested and brought to Clondalkin Garda Station for questioning. He had not been arrested in connection with Patrick Lawlor, but during the interview he started to talk about the missing teenager. It was the breakthrough the team had been waiting for. He brought Padraig Kennedy out to an area beside the ninth lock of the Grand Canal and pointed out where he believed Patrick was buried.

During that January Dolores had been starting to get a feeling, a physical sensation from her head to her toes. Part of her thought it might be sheer exhaustion from the worry and anguish of Patrick's disappearance.

A week before he was found she had a vivid dream. In the dream, she woke in the night and he was standing over her.

He was perfect, without a blemish, wearing a white tracksuit. She said, 'God, Patrick, where were you?' Then sleep dragged her down again. When she woke in her dream again, he was sitting on the floor almost in the foetal position, with his head down at his knees. She dreamed she woke a third time, and this time he was standing up again.

Later that week she found out her son Anthony's girlfriend was pregnant. That must have been what the kid was trying to tell me by sitting on the floor, she thought.

On Friday, 25 January 2002, she got an 8.00am phone call from Padraig Kennedy. They were going on a search for the body, he told her. This was not the first time she had received this call, and she would routinely go to work as normal rather than get her and all the family's hopes up. 'Don't go to work,' the detective told her. 'Make sure there's someone with you and keep the mobile on.' At that she broke down. 'Don't be crying, Dolores,' he said. 'I'll ring you back at half-one.'

She put the phone on the table and started walking from room to room in the house. Then the thought came to her, 'Oh my God, today's the day.' She rang her sister to ask her to come around.

As she looked out her window it started to rain. She looked at Patrick's photograph on the table and started to give out to him. 'Do something,' she urged him. 'Do something to show us where you are. I don't think I can take this much longer.' Her son grinned back at her.

She walked into the other room and looked out the front window. Suddenly, despite the rain, there was a gleam in the sky. Later Padraig Kennedy told her he noticed the same burst of sunshine. God, Patrick, that's where you are, isn't it? Dolores thought.

At half-one the call came: 'We still haven't got him, but hang on, hang in there,' the detective told her.

Later that afternoon her mobile rang again. 'I'm on my way,' Padraig Kennedy said to her. 'Tell me you found him,' she said. The detective wouldn't answer. Then her hall door opened and he came in, his mobile phone to his ear. 'We have him.'

For Dolores it was the same feeling as she had had more than twenty years earlier. 'It was like when he was born and he was taken, and then they gave him back to me. It was exactly like that day all over again. The first time Patrick was handed to me into life, wrapped in a blanket, and the second time Patrick was carried to me into death, a container of bones in a coffin.'

A question about Patrick's teeth banished any last doubts about the body for Dolores and her eldest daughter Mary. 'Did Patrick have anything wrong with his teeth?' Padraig Kennedy asked her as soon as he arrived in. Mother and daughter looked at each other. Patrick had a chip out of one of his front teeth. It was him.

Two days later they brought Dolores up to the site at the ninth lock where they had taken him out of the ground. Everyone was upset, including the younger gardaí who had worked on the case. Dolores found she couldn't cry, and spent her time comforting everyone else. Her whole system was flooded with the relief of finding him. There was no room for any other emotion. It was only later that the pain set in – the pain of not being able to hold his hand and comfort him in his dying moments, of not being able to see his remains before they were buried forever.

At the morgue in Marino she went to have some time alone

with him. Padraig Kennedy told her to stand against a wall in the prefab room and put her head resting against it on a certain spot. 'Patrick is in the vault behind you,' he said. They stayed in the room for over an hour and said a decade of the rosary.

It was thirteen weeks after he was found before the body was released for Patrick's funeral. Dolores worried about her kids' reaction. They had never seen a dead body or a coffin, or been to a funeral. On May Day 2002, she went to collect the remains and organised the children to wait for her outside the funeral home.

They had already chosen the coffin from a brochure Dolores had shown them, to try to involve them in the whole process of burying their young brother. When the coffin arrived into the viewing cubicle they were agog. Patrick's daughter Shanice was there and started to ask to see her father. In the cubicle next to them a woman was sitting with her loved one, the lid of the coffin off. 'Why can't we take the lid off?' Dolores' kids and her granddaughter clamoured. 'He's asleep,' Dolores kept telling them.

But this explanation was not enough for the children. 'But that woman's lid is off,' they said. 'Nanny, I want to see me daddy,' Shanice said. 'That lady's lid is off the coffin.'

So she had to tell them. 'Look, Patrick is in a little container in the coffin, and it's just bones. That's why we can't have the lid off.' She put her hand under the wooden coffin and felt the chill coming off the body after its removal from the vault. She told the children to feel the underside of the coffin and that seemed to satisfy them. The clamour to have the coffin open died down. Whenever anyone came in after that they would say: 'Feel underneath the coffin. It's freezin'.'

The reaction of the community in Ballyfermot was overwhelming. For Dolores it was a strange time. People would come up to her to say how delighted they were that he had been found, and then apologise as if they had said the wrong thing. 'I know what you mean,' she would say to them. She had a large funeral to organise and did not have time to think about her own reaction.

The priest on the day of the funeral talked about the horse that Patrick once owned, called Dizzy. At the mention of the horse's name one of her brood started giggling, and the giggle soon spread down the pew to the other kids. Dolores bit her lip, hoping that people would not think badly of them as the laughter echoed around the church. The kids were wired, laughing one minute and crying the next with the strangeness of it all. But she knows Patrick, a giggler himself, would not have wanted it any other way.

The children have reacted in different ways to the murder. Dolores sees her boys struggle with an anger that spills into the smallest arguments, blowing them out of proportion. Her daughters are less angry. Like her, they are more consumed with a feeling that they should have been there to protect Patrick. Dolores began grieving him shortly after he disappeared, knowing from that time that he was dead. For the children though, their brother's death only became a reality when his body was found.

Counselling is not automatically offered to children bereaved by violent death in Ireland. A lack of child bereavement services adds to a long waiting list for counselling. Victim Support has called for immediate free counselling to be offered to children bereaved by murder, available nationwide and, if possible, provided in the family home.

In a child's life, a six-month wait can seem like forever after the shock of a murder. For Dolores's children there was a wait of more than three years while they tried to come to terms with their brother's disappearance.

Then they went through his return, his funeral and a final farewell. Even after the burial, there was still a trial to face.

The eighth of December 2003, the Feast of the Immaculate Conception, was the date set for the trial of Gary Clarke. For Dolores the date was significant. She felt that Our Lady had given Patrick safely to her when he was born, and had helped to bring him back to her after he disappeared. Now the trial was to be held on her day.

As is common with court cases, the trial date was changed. It was Monday, 15 December, when Gary Clarke eventually stood up before Judge Paul Carney in the Central Criminal Court.

Until days before the case began, Dolores did not know whether Clarke would plead guilty or fight the charge. He was charged with a little-used criminal charge under a section of the act that deals with murder. Clarke was charged with acting to impede the arrest of a man responsible for the manslaughter of Patrick Lawlor. By the time the case opened it was clear that Clarke was pleading guilty.

Counsel for the State read a portion of Clarke's statement to the court. The heroin addict told gardaí in his statement that he had been walking along the canal on a night in January 1999 when he saw Patrick Lawlor and another man walking ahead of him.

Their voices started getting louder as a row broke out and Clarke said he caught up with them and told them, 'Stop acting the bollocks and keep fucking walking.' Then he said he 'heard a sound like a box', and saw the other man standing over Patrick with what looked like a boulder in his hand. He described the boulder as a large rock, but not so large that you could not hold it in one hand.

For reasons that Dolores and her family will never understand, and despite what he had witnessed, Clarke kept silent for three years about the whereabouts of Patrick's body.

Despite speculation about high-powered drug feuds and murderous drug barons, Patrick's death was merely the result of a violent and thuggish attack on a lonely canal path on a dark January night. His involvement with drugs led him to be in the wrong place at the wrong time, and in the brutal world of addiction there were no friendly faces to help him out of trouble.

Dolores feels that elements of the media judged her son before anyone knew why or how he had died. The only difference between his death and other random violent killings was that his body was hidden to cover up the crime; Dolores and her children had to wait three anguished years to find out what had happened to him.

His disappearance left a vacuum out of which theories about gangland assassinations emerged. Some of the coverage added injury to the hurt Dolores was already feeling.

She began to make use of the media, putting out appeals for information around the time of Patrick's birthday, Shanice's birthday and the anniversaries of his disappearance. One reporter, Yvonne Kinsella from the *Mirror*, became a friend and came to sit with her the morning they were looking for his body by the canal.

Dolores feels a lot of anger about Patrick's death. She feels that if they had attacked Patrick and then left him there and sent for help, she might at least have been able to be with him when he died. She might have been able to hold his hand in a hospital bed. Angry thoughts about what she would be capable of doing to his killer and the man who helped to bury him come to her at times. She pushes them away. She needs to keep peace and calm in her head for the sake of her children. The family has now moved house and started a new life.

Justice Paul Carney sentenced Gary Clarke to five years in prison for what he described as 'incalculable and unpardonable callousness'. Patrick Lawlor's loving family had experienced three years of 'untold suffering', the judge said, not knowing if the teenager was alive or dead. Clarke's silence for those years meant Patrick had been deprived of a civilised burial.

Dolores wanted to be in court for Patrick that Monday morning. She wanted to know why he died and was left where he was. His killing still does not make any sense.

'I hope every time they close their eyes and open their eyes that he's in front of them and they'll live with that for the rest of their lives.'

After his body was found she thought they might remove the memorial to his disappearance from the peace garden in Ballyfermot. But the priest was adamant that it should remain.

A second smaller piece of memorial granite has been added below it. It sits like an extra paragraph onto the end of the story of Patrick Lawlor's short life. Its words are a brief and eloquent testimony to his mother's three-year struggle to bring him back from the black hole into which he disappeared that day: 'Finally at rest 25th January 2002.'

LIFE SENTENCE

For Dolores Lawlor and her family, the laying to rest of Patrick's remains has brought some kind of closure. But the pain continues. Living with the uncertainty for so long, along with the loss of a son, brother and father, has taken its toll on the family. Nightmares return, about how he was lost in a twilight world of addiction; how he died, his body lying in a hole in the ground, cut off from his family. For Dolores it is a pain that she and her family will have to carry for the rest of their lives.

The case is still open. The truth of Patrick Lawlor's death has yet to be discovered.

Chapter 5

It took a clear mind
to do what he did

There are heartbreaking things left behind in her room. The tidy, bright space, with its lavender-painted walls and sloping eaves, was where she loved to be. It is a place of girlhood and womanhood, a room full of traces of who she was and who she could have become.

There is the furry toy seal still sitting at the end of her bed; the CD-ROM of careers information resting on top of her neat college folders. In the walk-in wardrobe her clothes hang as she left them. The satin cushions on the window seat are arranged in a row. A copy of the book she had been reading, *McCarthy's Bar*, is on the dressing table.

It was into here, Nichola Sweeney's comfortable, warm room, that Peter Whelan walked shortly after 10.55pm on the night of Saturday, 27 April 2002, with two kitchen knives tucked into his waistband, their shafts hidden under a hooded top. She was putting on her make-up in the en-suite bathroom when he stepped into the room. Her friend Sinead O'Leary was sitting at the top of Nichola's bed, using a heated tongs to curl her hair. In the space of a few minutes Nichola lay dying on the floor. Sinead was terrified and bleeding profusely from multiple stab wounds, locked in a downstairs bathroom in the dark, trying not to sob and to keep her ragged breathing quiet so he would not find her.

Later, the garda technical team would find Nichola's finger-prints and her blood on the panes of the dormer window in her bedroom, signs of Nichola's desperate attempts to get away from Peter Whelan and his knife.

Later still, her parents John and Josephine Sweeney would sit in a coroner's court in Cork and listen in horror to the medical evidence that took away the small comfort they had of believing their only daughter had died instantly. Professor John Harbison's evidence told them, in cold, clinical detail, that it would have taken four or five minutes for her lungs to fill with blood from a stab wound to her heart and for her to suffocate to death.

Whelan took nothing, disturbed nothing and broke nothing outside of the bedroom in Underwood House, the large comfortable family home in Rochestown, five miles from Cork city centre. He padded soundlessly down the long corridor from the back door to the stairs, pausing only to flick the light switches off and plunge the downstairs into darkness. He followed the sounds of voices up the stairs and along the corridor to the end bedroom.

On his way he passed family photographs and sketches of Nichola and her brothers. At the top of the stairs he might have glanced at the large, framed photograph of Nichola and her parents. She is pictured as a baby, sitting in her mother's arms and grinning toothlessly at the camera. Nichola used to cringe at that photograph, at her chubby baby cheeks. It made her look fat, she'd say to her dad.

The pictures stayed on their hooks as Peter Whelan passed them by that night, once on his way to the room and again on his way back out. The chaos of Whelan's attack was confined to Nichola's bedroom, the upstairs landing and the wooden staircase where Sinead bled as she fled for her life.

When the garda technical team left the house, friends of the Sweeneys organised a clean-up. A scene-of-crime service to clean up a murder scene is not offered by the State in the case of a murder in a family home. By the time John and Josephine moved back into the house, the carpets and bedding, and anything else destroyed by the blood, had been replaced. Nichola's belongings were cleaned so that the traces of what had happened would not greet her grieving parents.

In the weeks after his daughter's murder John Sweeney found himself going from room to room in the house and opening drawers and cupboards. Each time he opened something it surprised him to see the things inside neat and tidy, just as they had been when Nichola was still alive.

All this order and neatness made no sense in a world where Peter Whelan could walk into John Sweeney's home and stab his only daughter to death. If the ordinary world of things and belongings adequately reflected what had happened that Saturday night, it would be as if a maelstrom had swept through the house, wrecking everything in its wake.

For John, the ordinariness of everything was a profound shock after the enormity of what had happened. There was a surreal quality about how real things were. He and his wife's minds and lives were in turmoil, and yet the house where Nichola was killed was so perfect, so nice and so normal. When they thought about it rationally, it was only right that everything would be as it was before they left. The tidiness and order had survived her death. But they were a horrible reminder of a time when everything was still in its rightful place – belongings in their allotted drawers and Nichola still alive and well.

It was Nichola who had chosen Underwood House. She was drawn to it. The house offered everything a horse-mad teenage girl who loved countryside, space and light could wish for. She was fifteen when they first saw it.

Nichola was born in Cork in October 1981. The Sweeneys' delight at her arrival was even more intense than the usual joy of a first baby, because Nichola had been Josephine's fourth pregnancy. There had been three miscarriages before she was born and the gynaecologists were not confident that Josephine could carry a baby to term.

In the Bons Secours Hospital the cycle of pregnancy and loss ended and Nichola Jayne Sweeney became the light of their lives. She came six weeks before her due date. There was an anxious two weeks as their tiny baby girl recovered in intensive care. Then she thrived.

When she was twelve months old John and Josephine moved to London to start a family pub business. So Nichola lived in Highgate in north London for her first fifteen years as her parents worked hard running the family pub, the Archway Tavern, and expanding into other London pubs. Her younger brother Sean was born in London. The family travelled home at least once a year, usually to the children's grandparents in John and Josephine's home parishes of Glenbeigh and Beaufort, County Kerry.

It was Easter 1997 when the family came property-hunting to Cork. Friends had heard from a local estate agent that Underwood House was to go on the market. The large, handsome dormer bungalow was set into the hillside in Rochestown on five acres of garden, with panoramic views over Cork harbour and Hop Island laid out in front of it.

It was a house where it seemed Josephine would never have need for the net curtains she disliked. It seemed that only the birds could peer in through the windows in the light-filled property, standing as it was above the road overlooking everything. From the house, Nichola could see the equestrian centre on Hop Island where she rode her beloved horses. As soon as Nichola saw the house she was certain.

That day they had looked at ten different properties, Underwood House being the first. 'Gosh, Mum and Dad, this is definitely the house,' Nichola told them as soon as she saw it. Josephine liked another property on the Model Farm Road. In the end it was Nichola's delight that swayed them. Now John feels it was almost as if her fate was laid out. Everything pulled her towards Underwood.

That September they moved in, dovetailing the move with the start of the school year. Nichola was enthusiastic about the move back to Ireland. Sean was less eager, having grown up in London and become a committed Tottenham Hotspur fan. For Nichola, London was too noisy and frantic. She felt safer and more at ease in the quiet beauty of Rochestown, and the country she had always loved as home.

The family kept a flat in Highgate where John and Josephine based themselves when they were running the pubs. The option was there to move back to London if the family did not settle in Cork.

When their parents went on trips to London, Nichola and Sean stayed with cousins on the opposite side of Cork city. But Nichola loved to be in her own home, surrounded by her own things. Although she was quiet and a little shy, she was independent. By the age of nineteen, she would stay in Underwood House with Sean, who was then sixteen. She was never afraid of being in the big house on her own. There were eight-foot high walls, electronic gates and a CCTV security system. At weekends a school friend or two would often come to stay with her.

By buying in 1997, before the property boom took a real hold, the Sweeneys got a relative bargain. For the family it was like a dream come true. A surprise addition to the family, baby Christopher, was born after the move home to Cork. Nichola doted on her new brother.

There were eight houses in the hamlet of Underwood, built along the cul-de-sac that snaked up from the main Rochestown road. The Sweeneys got to know three of the families, including two elderly neighbours. On the small monitor that relayed pictures from the camera at their gate, they used to see a garda squad car driving past occasionally. They always assumed this was just a routine patrol, checking on the well-being of their elderly neighbours.

It was only afterwards they learned that the squad car was usually the gardaí visiting the home of Peter Whelan, a young neighbour around the same age as Nichola.

After the murder John Sweeney was trying to understand what had happened, the how and the why of his daughter's senseless death. The soft-spoken Kerryman spent days trying to put himself inside the mind of the man who had killed his daughter. For the world to make sense he needed to find a reason for the murder. He started by trying to find out whether Nichola's path could have crossed Whelan's and sparked something.

He asked his son Sean if something had happened on the bus to give Whelan a grudge against them. They had not shared bus journeys, Sean told him. Sean and Nichola left for school on the 8.00am bus to Cork city centre; Whelan's bus would take him in the opposite direction, to Passage West, at a quarter to nine. 'Would he have got some silly notion that you were laughing at him on the bus at weekends?' John asked Sean. No, all Whelan's friends were in Passage West and, with a three-year age gap between him and Sean, they were never pals.

John had met Peter Whelan on just two occasions over the four years that they lived at Underwood. Once he had given him and another young lad a lift into town. He had asked Whelan his name and who he was during the brief car journey. Another time Whelan's mother rang to say that the trees at the back of the Sweeney house had grown so high they were interfering with their satellite signal. John went down to the Whelans' house and she came out with Peter. They pointed up to where the trees were, had some neighbourly chat and John duly trimmed the tops of the trees.

Sometimes Whelan would walk by the gate with the family dog, a King Charles spaniel, as John was gardening. 'Hello, Peter,' John would say. The young man always replied politely, 'Hello, Mr Sweeney.'

Due to the layout of the cul-de-sac, the Sweeneys never passed the Whelans' house to get to their own home, even though they lived so close. Despite the fact that he lived only two houses away, Peter Whelan was virtually a stranger to them.

For John Sweeney, the five acres of shrubbery and lawns with the driveway curving round to the house provided a haven from his business responsibilities whilst home from his London-based business. On summer evenings when she came home from school to find her dad working in his garden, Nichola used to say, 'Dad, you must be delighted I got you to buy this house.'

John Sweeney now thinks of Peter Whelan as a time bomb that was ticking alongside their happy existence.

Nichola finished at Scoil Mhuire in Cork city in 1999, leaving the secondary school with a wide circle of new friends. She enrolled in a business degree course at Skerries College and got herself a part-time job at Brown's Café in the Brown Thomas department store in Cork city.

On Saturday, 27 April 2002, she worked her shift as usual at the café and left for home after the shop closed at 6.00pm. Exams were looming and she planned a quiet night in with her friend Sinead O'Leary – a meal, some study and then a video that Sinead would bring.

That evening she rang her parents' flat in Highgate at around 8.00pm and chatted with both John and Josephine. She would usually ring them two or three times a day, often just to chat. Nichola and Josephine's relationship had an ease and closeness that often made them seem more like sisters than mother and daughter.

That April Saturday night, both of them had been glued to the ITV game show 'Stars in Their Eyes', because a young woman they knew from Cork was appearing on the show that night, in the grand final. The Cobh contestant was doing a Tina Turner impersonation, and mother and daughter were cheering at the screen for her, Nichola at home in Underwood and Josephine in the flat in Highgate.

Again, at 10.30 that night, Nichola rang the flat in London. The local girl had come second in the competition and Nichola and her mother agreed it had been a disappointment. Josephine was busy with Christopher, trying to settle him into bed, so she told Nichola she would ring her back as soon as the child was asleep.

In the meantime, Nichola and Sinead had spoken to friends in town. They had decided to abandon the plans for the video and go out instead. Upstairs in Nichola's room they started getting ready. Sean had gone out with a friend to the other side of the city.

It was months before John Sweeney could sit down with Sinead and talk to her about what happened next. Her recall was total. It was as if the danger she was in during Whelan's attack had flooded her senses with heightened sensitivity. She remembered every detail vividly.

She was sitting at the head of Nichola's bed doing her hair when Peter Whelan stepped through the open bedroom doorway into the room. Sinead was startled first and stood up, thinking he must be a friend of Sean's. Then she realised this was no friend as Whelan lunged at her and punched her to the ground, kicking and stamping on her as she lay crouched into the side of the bed trying to protect herself. Nichola dropped everything and came out from the bathroom disturbed by the noise. It was only then that Whelan lifted his hoodie and showed them the two knives in his waistband.

Then Whelan started stabbing Sinead. Nichola was screaming at Whelan to stop. During his attack on her, Sinead remembers that he kept staring at Nichola with an evil smile. He stabbed Sinead twenty times, most of the wounds to her arms and upper body. The attack was so ferocious that he broke his first knife on her.

As he attacked her friend, he was placed between Nichola and the doorway. There was no way she could escape. Looking up from his first victim he came towards her and she rushed to lock herself into the bathroom. Whelan kicked a hole in the bottom of the door and forced the door in on her before she could get it locked. As he attacked Nichola, Sinead managed to get herself up. She scrambled and half-fell her way downstairs, finding the bathroom off the hall despite the darkness and locking herself in. She was alone, badly injured and terrified that Whelan would find her.

The events that unfolded in the hours that follow highlight the need for comprehensive training to be given to people who have to break the terrible news of a murder to family members. Trauma experts agree that the moment of hearing the news of a murder remains with someone for the rest of their lives. And the way that news is broken can have an effect on the subsequent healing process. The Sweeneys, especially their teenage son Sean, heard about Nichola's death in dreadful circumstances.

Just as she had promised, Josephine rang her daughter back after she had settled Christopher to sleep that night. It was 11.20pm, less than a hour after she had been chatting happily about the TV show with her daughter. Although she would not know it for certain until hours later, by the time she dialled Nichola's number again Nichola was dead and nothing would ever be the same again.

Sinead answered Josephine's call. Showing remarkable strength and composure, the nineteen-year-old student managed to tell Josephine that there had been a break-in. Nichola was hurt, Sinead said, and the Gardaí had come. She handed the phone to a garda to speak to Josephine. The garda told Nichola's mother he had only just arrived. He would find out what had happened and phone her back.

Josephine hung up and rang the Archway Tavern where John was working. 'Come up quick. Something terrible's after happening,' she told him. Immediately he thought something had happened to Christopher in the flat. 'Oh no, it's at home in Ireland,' Josephine told him.

On the short drive back, John's mind was racing – he wondered if Sean had had a car accident, as his son had just started driving. Then he wondered if Nichola's new pet, Buzz the dog, had run out under a car.

When Josephine met him at the door and told him it was Nichola he was stunned. The idea that something had happened to his loving, sensible daughter had never crossed his mind. He began to phone the house. The ringing tone sounded for what seemed like hours. Both phones – the landline and Nichola's mobile – rang out for at least twenty minutes.

In desperation he dialled the number of Douglas Garda Station. With the phones unmanned in Douglas, the call was diverted to Togher. A woman garda took his query and said she would phone back. He gave her both landline and mobile numbers, so that she could reach him even as he kept trying the house.

All the while, as John frantically tried to make contact with Underwood, he and Josephine pictured Nichola hurt somehow, maybe slapped or punched by some intruder intent on robbery. Maybe she had broken a leg or sprained a wrist during the intrusion, they thought.

After many attempts, Nichola's phone was answered by a male voice. It was a garda at the scene. 'What's happened my daughter?' John asked. He was told to ring the University Hospital in Cork. John became alarmed. 'Tell me what are her injuries?' he asked. 'I'm sorry, I'm sorry,' the man answered, 'ring UCH.' John's heart started to beat faster. 'Is she unconscious? Has she got a broken leg?' At each question the man at the other end kept repeating, 'I'm sorry.'

Suddenly John's mind plunged to the worst possible thought. 'I'm going to ask you a very simple question,' he said. 'Is my daughter dead or alive?' All the unfortunate man on the other end of the phone could say was, 'I'm sorry. I'm sorry. I'm sorry.' From that moment John knew the worst but he felt himself going into denial. Just then another phone rang in the flat and he blanked out that previous conversation and went through the whole routine again.

A more senior officer was on the phone as a result of John Sweeney's call to Togher Garda Station. The man told John that the most urgent priority was to get over from London. It was close to midnight and John knew the earliest flight was not for over seven hours from Stansted.

'I really need to know from you what is the situation with my daughter,' he said, as if the previous conversation had not happened. 'You really need to come over straight away,' was the response. John asked him the same question he had asked the first garda: 'Is my daughter dead or alive?' He got the same response – the advice to get home. He thinks now it was a coded way of telling him the worst without voicing the words down a phone line.

In the meantime Sean Sweeney, at home in Cork, was also learning the awful news in stages. He was with his friend Conor who had just collected him that night, and they drove back to Rochestown from Bishopstown after getting a call from his father in London. He got to the bottom of the driveway and found the entrance sealed off and two gardaí manning the scene. He told the gardaí it was his house and that his sister was there. He was told that no-one would be allowed up, as there was a girl dead and another girl injured. On hearing this shocking news a wave of fear engulfed him. When he got his breath back he asked who had been killed. He was told to go to the hospital to get information.

With his friend, Sean drove across the city to the hospital and approached the desk at the casualty unit. The two staff members were appalled to hear the nature of their query. A woman went away for a few minutes and returned. Before she spoke, Sean spotted a name written in biro on the back of her hand. 'Sinead' read the hastily written scrawl. They asked him what his sister's name was. 'Nichola Sweeney,' he told them. They said that all they could confirm was that the girl being treated for injuries was Sinead O'Leary.

In hysterics, Sean rang his father. It was the first time that John Sweeney had real verbal confirmation of what had happened. 'Dad, Nichola's dead.'

John Sweeney does not blame the gardaí. It is human nature, he reasons, not to want to deliver bad news. He saves his anger and blame for Peter Whelan.

There is no emotional equivalent to the death of a child. The parent who watches their child being buried, whether that child is infant or adult, is going down a path that nature never intended. The order of things is turned on its head. The loss is immeasurable.

When that child is a murder victim the emotional impact is even more devastating. 'Why did Nichola die?' is the question with which John and Josephine still struggle. In the case of a murder, the anger at a world in which your child should have been safe from harm has a focus point.

John Sweeney has focused his mind on Peter Whelan.

Two days after the murder he sat down to write a few brief words for Nichola's funeral mass in Glenbeigh, County Kerry. It would be the last time they would share a room with her and he wanted to say something. On a page he wrote that he forgave Nichola's killer and expressed sympathy towards his family. When a friend saw it, he counselled John against saying this so soon in the numbness of shock. John took his advice and deleted the words.

Instead of forgiveness he searched for understanding. Now he feels that giving his forgiveness that day would have been ridiculous. He is adamant now, after attempting to understand, that Whelan's actions that Saturday night were not actions of madness but of evil.

He believes that when people hear a description of the case – a young man breaking into a nearby house chosen at random, killing one young woman and almost killing another – they have visions of a lunatic rushing into the house in a frenzy of violent intent.

The London-based Kerry publican set about trying to get inside the head of the young man who lived quietly beside them for four years and then, in a random act of savagery, murdered his daughter. He discovered that on the night of the attack Whelan was already facing charges over a serious assault on young women at a New Year's Eve party. On the night of Nichola's murder, Whelan had been thrown out of a pub after trying to attack a barman. On his walk home with his friend Stacy McCarthy he saw a young man walking ahead. Whelan picked up a rock to attack him. At that stage McCarthy got a lift on the road and Whelan was left alone. He dropped the rock and cut up to his house to get his knives. Once there, he was delayed when his father gave him summonses that had been served by the gardaí over the New Year's Eve attack. By the time Whelan got back down onto the main road the young man, the random target of his anger, had gone.

Behind him were the stone walls of Underwood House, the place that Nichola Sweeney had chosen as her safe new home in Ireland. Whelan made a snap decision. He later told gardaí that he chose Underwood House at random. He climbed over the walls, walked up the steep driveway in the dark and tried the front door. Walking around the outside of the house and peering in the windows, he was able to ascertain there was no-one downstairs in the house. He tried the back door and found it unlocked.

As he made his way through the kitchen and along the corridor, he must have followed the sound of voices. He walked quietly along and did what John Sweeney believes it took a very clear mind to do. He turned off all the lights after him, leaving the downstairs in darkness. It was only when he saw the two young women on their own in the room that he revealed his weapons. Until that point John thinks he was biding his time. With the knives hidden, he could have made up an excuse for being in the house if it had happened that more of the family had been at home.

Then the attacks unfolded and Sinead was lucky to escape alive. By the time Sinead O'Leary had given her detailed description to the gardaí who arrived on the scene that night, Peter Whelan was standing in the driveway, in a new set of clothes, as if he were a concerned neighbour. When gardaí approached him to arrest him, he is said to have told them he was 'sorry he didn't do more,' which they took to mean that he would have liked to have killed Sinead as well.

As the murder trial approached, the Sweeneys were anxious that Whelan would not fight the charges. As far as they were concerned, Nichola's character could be called into question if he tried to escape a murder conviction. Whelan could have claimed to have had some kind of relationship with her. They wanted the world to know that Nichola never knew her killer or had any dealings with him.

The trial opened in the Four Courts in Dublin in the week before Christmas 2002. To the Sweeneys' relief, Whelan pleaded guilty to the two charges – the murder of Nichola Sweeney and the attempted murder of Sinead O'Leary.

Details of the attacks were read into the court record. High Court Judge Paul Carney imposed the mandatory life sentence for murder and a fifteen-year sentence for the attempted murder. Usually such sentences are imposed to run concurrently, the fifteen years taken as part of the life sentence. In a highly unusual move, Judge Carney added the fifteen years on to the end of the life sentence, to run consecutively. Due to what he called the 'horrific circumstances of this outrage', he gave Whelan, in effect, life and another fifteen years.

Whelan was led out in handcuffs. A month later, the Sweeneys read that he had been taken to Cork Prison after his initial remand to Mountjoy. He was now sitting in a prison that was visible from their home. No-one had informed them that he had been sent to Cork Prison. They read about it in a newspaper report, along with the information that he was appealing the murder and attempted-murder sentences.

In May 2003 the Sweeneys were back in the Four Courts, to hear the case before the three-judge Court of Criminal Appeal over the legality of Judge Carney's sentence.

After hearing arguments that the imposition of a fifteen-year sentence on top of what was supposed to be a life sentence was an error in law, the court ruled that it was not the consecutive nature, but the order of the sentences that could be changed. In a move that the Sweeneys welcomed, the court ruled that Whelan must serve the fifteen years for attempted murder, and then begin his life sentence for murder.

Supreme Court Judge Adrian Hardiman said there was nothing disproportionate about the fifteen-year sentence, as the attack on Sinead O'Leary had been of the utmost savagery.

After the judgment was handed down, John Sweeney stood up in the body of the court and asked that the court would examine the issue of life sentence, as it was 'farcical'. Judge Hardiman said it was not for the court to undertake that work, and urged John Sweeney to take it up elsewhere.

The relief of having the trial over and the appeal dealt with in the best way they could have hoped is tempered with the knowledge that Whelan has continued his legal battles. In March 2004 Whelan's legal team went to the High Court to challenge the law requiring judges to hand down a mandatory life sentence for murder. The lawyers argued that a mandatory life sentence was a breach of the Constitution and the European Convention of Human Rights.

Whelan's legal team argued that the effects of the reversal of the sentencing structure – giving him the fifteen years and then life – were unknown, and it was not certain that Whelan would be able to apply to the Parole Board for early or temporary release on licence.

Mr Justice Quirke directed that the constitutional challenge be dealt with by way of plenary summons.

At the end of March 2004 the Court of Criminal Appeal rejected as 'utterly without merit' a separate bid by Whelan to reopen his appeal. The three-judge court also refused to refer the matter to the Supreme Court.

At the time of writing, the constitutional challenge was still proceeding and the expectation is that if Whelan fails, he will take an action to the European Court of Human Rights.

John Sweeney has tried to be in court each and every time Whelan's legal actions are being dealt with. The continuing battles are exhausting and frustrating for him.

Nichola Sweeney would never have supported the death penalty, and neither do her parents. What they want is for Peter Whelan to remain in prison for life. It is a situation of justice, John Sweeney argues. He believes there is no justice in Whelan being allowed to walk free when their daughter is gone from them. And there is also the real risk, John Sweeney believes, that he might do the same to another family and destroy their lives also.

After the appeal was finished, John and Josephine put together the Nichola Sweeney Foundation, primarily to campaign for a life sentence to mean life, and also to provide support for other families of murder victims.

A website, www.nicholasweeneyfoundation.org, provides a tribute to their murdered daughter in pictures and words and they hope other families will find it helpful. They think they will soon have to move from Underwood House. It is still a place of peace and beauty, despite the awful events of Saturday, 27 April 2002.

'Death is often associated more with its location than with the person responsible,' John says. 'The house never did anything to Nichola. She loved it immensely. The person that killed Nichola is really the person responsible. In every other way, apart from the terrible thing that happened here, this was our home.'

Nichola's room remains as it was the day she died. The door that her baby brother would knock on when he toddled down to see her is open. But her parents sleep downstairs.

The house does not haunt them, but living so close to Peter Whelan's family does. Every Saturday morning at the same time they see the car passing their gate as his family goes to see him in prison.

Whelan has never expressed remorse to the Sweeneys. In court he said nothing.

Josephine Sweeney sees a counsellor regularly to try and deal with the aftermath of Nichola's death. Her husband tried counselling, but could not relate to the counsellor's suggestion that everyone was capable of evil. His anger is quiet and con-trolled and has driven him to try to delve deeply into the mind of his former neighbour.

No State provision of counselling has been offered. The ses-sions are paid for privately by the Sweeneys. Like many other families, they have been left to pick up the pieces themselves.

'In many ways we don't want to let go of the emotion. Typically, when you're trying to sleep at night or when you wake in the morning, Nichola immediately comes to your mind. Suddenly there's almost a defence mechanism that says "Stop thinking about her," and you feel guilty even about that. You feel that some day you'll condition your body to push her out of your mind. It's one way of dealing with it. But I always stop my defensive measures of dealing with it, because it would be wholly disrespectful to her. We never want to forget her. We never will.'

Chapter 6

My sister with the beautiful blue eyes

Stella and Sylvia were a double act. Stella plaited her baby sister's hair and got her out of scrapes at the Loreto school in Kilkenny, the 'coldest place in Ireland', where the sisters were boarders. Later they grew up to share a flat for years and work in the civil service. Sylvia sparkled. She was sharp and charming, with no patience for people she deemed boring or tedious. There were dances, tennis matches, friends and boyfriends – Stella doing her best to impress the men who called and Sylvia pouring scorn on them from a height.

'Why wouldn't I want to talk about her?' Stella said on my first phonecall. 'I should be writing a book about her myself. To everyone else she is just some dead old woman.'

As far as Stella is concerned, Sylvia was four things: the youngest, the prettiest, the brightest and mammy's pet. To the rest of the country she wears the label of a psychiatric patient who died in the shockingly brutal double killing that became known as the Grangegorman murders.

The place where she died and Mark Nash – the man who confessed to her murder and then withdrew that confession – are both names that get more recognition than her own. Sylvia Sheils had a life before she took up residence, with two other women patients, in the small terraced house at Orchard View.

But the person she was when she died means that few people know her as anything other than an institutionalised victim.

Even her surname has been lost in the flurry of public interest in her case. It was a mistake that has been repeated hundreds of times, whenever the case is mentioned. Her Donegal surname Sheils became 'Shields' in the initial reports of her death, and Sylvia has been known by that name ever since. It was a simple and understandable error, but one that means the historical record of her death is consigned to a misspelt name.

The parents of English toddler James Bulger, who was killed by two boys after they abducted him in a shopping centre in one of Britain's most notorious murders, never called their son Jamie. The British press christened the child Jamie almost immediately after his death. It was a move to enhance the already-heartbreaking idea of his childish vulnerability. After his death he was referred to widely as Jamie Bulger and the name has remained in the public consciousness.

For different reasons, Sylvia is remembered by another name to the one that she had all her life.

Grangegorman was a long way from where Sylvia spent her childhood. Breffni House in Killiney was the comfortable address for Sylvia's father – an inspector of taxes – along with his wife, three daughters and a son.

In 1930s Dublin the life of a senior civil servant was a quiet, orderly existence. Killiney was virtually the countryside. With no car and no telephone, the railway provided the link to the city and nearby Dalkey, where the children – Clare, Stella, Rourke and Sylvia – went to school.

Memories of childhood for Stella are a mix of summer days on the beach and winter days spent bundled up coats, hats and scarves, trudging to the station for the train to school, and the long trudge home again in the evenings.

In 1945 Stella asked her father for a special gift for her twelfth birthday. She wanted a family portrait. The handsome black-and-white photograph taken in the studio of a local photographer was the last time her family was pictured together. In the picture Sylvia looks like a carbon copy of her pretty mother, standing beside her and smiling at the camera. By September of that year their father had succumbed to stomach cancer and was dead.

Stella's mother worked hard to nurse her sick husband through his last months that summer. She would regularly kill a hen from the flock she kept in the back garden. By the end all he could eat was the broth.

Life for the four children was never the same again. Their mother had been a pupil at the Loreto on the Green, in the centre of Dublin, and loved books and reading thanks to her favourite teacher, a Loreto nun. Sister Mary Margaret had gone on to become mistress of schools at the Loreto in Kilkenny, and it was decided that this would be the best place for the children after their father's death. However, when they arrived in Kilkenny their mother's former teacher had moved to Bray.

Miles from home the three Sheils sisters – Clare, Stella and Sylvia, who at the age of six was the school's youngest boarder – shared a three-bed dorm. Sylvia was always in trouble. Stella rolled up her ribbons and plaited her hair and tried to keep her on the straight and narrow.

Even at the age of six, Sylvia had a strong personality and was doggedly argumentative. When a row started she would persist until she eventually wore down her opponent and got her own way.

The family funds ran out before Sylvia finished school, so she returned to Dublin, studied in the college on Kevin Street, qualified with flying colours as a draughtsman and got a job in the Valuation Office on Ely Place. Like her father, she was a civil servant, permanent and pensionable. But unlike him she was a woman in a man's world.

Women were not expected to stay long in their civil service jobs in the 1950s and 1960s. The accepted view was that women would work until they found a good husband. Marriage meant an automatic exit from the civil service under the marriage ban which remained in place until Ireland joined the EEC in 1973. Those women civil servants who stayed in the workforce were viewed with some pity by their male colleagues who rose through the ranks while the 'spinsters' continued to work at lower grades.

These were the women who watched increasingly younger men arrive, learn their trade with the help of their female colleagues and then automatically climb to the next rung of the promotion ladder. For decades the power structure was unchallenged. Women like Sylvia got left behind and became part of the furniture in civil service offices.

But for those early years Sylvia had Stella. The two sisters shared a flat on Elgin Road, in the Dublin Four embassy belt. The Sheils sisters were young and gregarious with a wide circle of friends.

Stella watched her lively, bright sister fall for a man in the office. The two would lunch together all week and then at weekends he pursued his own interests, which did not include Sylvia. The office crush was one of Sylvia's first disappointments in life.

Later there was another man whom she agreed to marry. But the engagement came to nothing.

In Elgin Road the two sisters had a dramatically different approach to dating and boyfriends. Stella would spend hours getting ready and worrying about what her date would think of her. Sylvia would laugh at her efforts, telling her the boyfriend was probably more nervous than she was. Stella felt that Sylvia thought she could take any boyfriend her older sister had. And she did, regularly, just to show she could. She didn't want them at all, she would tell Stella. They weren't worth taking, she said.

Then in 1970, the sisters' happy co-existence ended when Stella got married and moved out of the flat they had shared. In the following four years Stella had four children. Her busy life as a young mother meant little time to keep an eye on her baby sister.

It may have been a coincidence, but without her sister Sylvia went into a decline. She stopped socialising, then stopped going out at all and soon stopped eating and drinking and looking after herself. The flat in Elgin Road was gutted by fire and she moved to a flat on her own in Sandymount.

It was in Sandymount that the public health nurse was called. Stella got a call one day to tell her that Sylvia was unwell. Stella hardly recognised her sister. There was a dreadful scene that day. Sylvia knew what was happening and Stella had to sign her into the psychiatric facility at St Brendan's Hospital in Grangegorman. Sylvia held tightly to the mattress as they tried to take her away.

Another two times Stella would sign her sister in. After that she decided that if Sylvia did not want to live, she did not have the moral right to force her.

Sylvia had never actively tried to kill herself. Her attempts to die were by neglect. She would stop eating and refuse to leave the flat. It was as if she had neither the will to live nor the will to kill herself.

Stella asked her often if it was depression that she suffered. 'No,' Sylvia would answer. 'It's anxiety.' She thinks the mental health professionals eventually labelled her sister a schizophrenic.

Sylvia was withdrawn but aware. She shrank into herself over the years, her strangeness increasing along with her size as she piled on weight. She was living in a silence of her own making, but missed nothing that happened around her.

Stella once asked her what she would do when her money ran out. 'Sure, I'll die,' Sylvia said.

'Are you not afraid of dying?' Stella would ask. 'Everyone's afraid of dying.'

'No,' Sylvia would say, 'I'm only going back to be with Mammy.'

Stella believes it was with her mother as a child that Sylvia was at her happiest. She never found anyone in her adult life who loved her like her mother had. Mentally her younger sister just keeled over with the slow pain of life's disappointments.

Eventually Sylvia was admitted as a permanent patient to St Brendan's. She still worked in the Valuation Office, and left the hospital for work every day. But by then she had become quite strange. She refused to talk to people, keeping entirely to herself. She neglected herself, forgetting to eat or have a bath. Eventually she took early retirement, received a lump sum, and walked away from the draughtsman's desk that had been her first job.

The money did not last long, and private health insurance had not been a perk of her lower-grade civil service job. She was put into the public health system for psychiatric care. In the early 1980s she moved out to sheltered housing in Stanhope Street. Then, along with two other women, she moved into Orchard View, a terraced row of small houses adjoining St Brendan's Hospital in Dublin's north inner city. The houses were a step-down facility for patients who did not need full-time hospital care. She had a job in a local factory which had an employment arrangement with the hospital.

Although she was not institutionalised, Sylvia led a highly regimented life. There were no locks or bars on her windows, but she kept to a clockwork routine. She would leave the house at 8.00am, eat her lunch out and then return in the early evening. Every night the three women went to bed at the same time. Her year always ended with a visit to Stella for the weeks around Christmas.

For Stella's children the arrival of their aunt Sylvia was not a festive highlight. They used to laugh and make fun of her. On her bad days she was a black cloud that hung over their Christmas.

She had lost most of her hair and wore a tar-black wig. One day Frank, Stella's youngest boy, went up with Sylvia's cornflakes to give her breakfast in bed. He came screaming down the stairs, 'She's two heads,' he roared. 'One of them on the chair and one of them on the bed.'

Frank was her favourite nephew. Stella was amazed at her funeral to hear from people who knew Sylvia that she never stopped talking about Stella's four children, her two nieces and two nephews.

She was a familiar sight on the steep hill from Stella's house down to Tallaght village. Then it was a remote country road. Now it is surrounded by new housing estates. Wrapped in a huge brown fur coat, she would negotiate the icy slope in mid-winter. Neighbours saw her on the road. They couldn't miss her. She walked in the centre, so they had to stop and give her a lift.

She gained a lot of weight as the years went on and at Christmas she would sit in a chair in Stella's living room, talking to no-one and chain-smoking. But by the mid-1990s, her job had given her a new momentum – by the time of her death she would only go to visit Stella for a few nights at Christmas. She wanted to get back to the room of her own that she loved at Orchard View.

Over Christmas 1996, Sylvia came to stay as usual and admired a touch lamp Stella had bought. The bedside lamp came on when you touched the base. There was no need to go looking for the switch in the dark. Her sister said she would get one for her. Two days before Sylvia was murdered, Stella talked to her and told her she had bought the lamp, along with an extension lead to let her plug it in beside her bed. She had bath oils as well, as a treat for Sylvia.

Stella thought her sister was just starting to come back to herself. She was taking more of an interest in her appearance. Her co-workers were very good to her. A new chapter in her lonely existence seemed to be opening up.

On the morning of 7 March 1997, Stella Nolan switched on her bedside radio and heard the shocking news on the bulletin about the murder of two psychiatric patients at Grangegorman. She jumped up and telephoned a cousin. 'Could that be our Sylvie?' she said, not wanting to believe it. Her cousin telephoned the hospital and was told, yes, that Sylvia Sheils, their fifty-eight-year-old patient, was one of the victims.

There was no phone in the house at Orchard View. Stella drove to her brother Rourke's house in Phibsboro and the two of them went to Orchard View. They saw the Garda tape around the house where Sylvia had lived. On the RTÉ news that night, the cameraman's footage of the crime scene pictured the two of them walking up the pavement to look at the house. It was lunchtime before the gardaí came to Rourke's door to give him the news.

Stella's gut instinct was to go to the house and look at the scene, to try and decipher Sylvia's last moments, how she was attacked and how she reacted. She knew on which side of the bed her sister slept. But Stella was not allowed into the house. She still has not received any of her sister's personal belongings, six years after the murder.

A doctor asked her to bring a photograph of Sylvia to the morgue to help identify the body. She was not allowed to see her sister's body until it was laid out in the funeral home.

Sylvia had returned to the house the night before, just as she always did. Anne Mernagh, who also lived in the house, saw her before Anne left for bingo and again afterwards at around 11.40pm when she asked Sylvia for a wake-up call. While Anne Mernagh was out at bingo another patient, Edward Moloney, called to the door to deliver a message to Sylvia. She took the message and then closed the door.

Sometime in the middle of that March night, an intruder smashed a window and climbed into the house with its three sleeping occupants: Anne, Sylvia and Mary Callinan. He went into the kitchen and yanked open the kitchen drawers. He emptied two drawers of knives and a carving fork and walked up to the bedrooms. It appears that he first killed Mary Callinan, a sixty-one-year-old woman who was another long-term patient. He stabbed her more than thirty times in a frenzied attack, the like of which gardaí had never seen before. Apparently disturbed by the noise, Sylvia was half out of bed when he stabbed her in the chest and neck, cutting her throat. The murders were no clinical assassinations.

Stella believes her sister would have fought any attacker. She was not surprised to learn that Sylvia appeared to have put up a defence rather than being found lying prone. When details of the murders and the mutilation inflicted on the two women found their way into the newspapers, Stella felt haunted. Newspaper headlines screamed out about Hannibal Lector, knives left stuck in the bodies and pieces of the bodies missing.

Anne Mernagh had had a miraculous escape. Blood stains on her bedroom carpet showed that the murderer had walked into her room. She had taken some medication and fallen into a deep sleep with her personal cassette headphones on. She heard nothing of the horror that happened sometime between 11.40pm and just before 1.20am the next morning. Someone had stepped into her bedroom long enough to leave blood on her carpet and then turned and left the house, leaving her still sleeping and unharmed.

She was the first to find Sylvia, lying across her bed. She spoke to her friend before realising that she was dead and when she touched her she found that Sylvia was cold.

The Grangegorman murders gripped the country. The unprecedented savagery of the attacks and the fact that the women were psychiatric patients led firstly to speculation that another psychiatric patient had killed them.

For Stella the days and weeks that followed were filled with terror. She woke every night between two and four and lay looking at the ceiling, thinking about what had happened to Sylvia.

She quarrelled with relatives over how the family should respond to what had happened. One family member thought they should accept that Sylvia was dead and there was nothing that could be done. Stella is still angry that her sister lived in a house without a phone, alarm or panic button that might have afforded them more protection. With their clockwork routines, the vulnerable women were sitting targets.

Stella played Mozart's Great Mass every night, especially in those waking hours. Music and her family got her through the days and weeks that followed the murders.

She told her children that they did not have to come to Sylvia's funeral. She was particularly concerned that her eldest son, who was a teacher, would face difficulties with the children in his school if they knew it was his aunt who had been murdered. All four children insisted on coming with her to the funeral.

Stella could not talk to anyone about her feelings. And for her children, who only knew Sylvia as a chain-smoking presence in the living room at Christmas, Stella's grief was difficult to understand. They had not known their young, pretty aunt before her decline into silence and self-neglect.

As Sylvia's big sister, Stella had lost someone she had known almost all her life. The public understanding of loss and grief often overlooks the siblings of a murder victim, focusing on the parents, spouse or children as those most deserving of sympathy and support. The fact that she learned of her sister's murder through a radio news bulletin exacerbated the hurt and shock of the event.

Trauma experts agree that the way a person is informed about such a shocking event as the murder of a loved one has a large impact on the recovery process. Although the time after finding out a family member is dead can be a blur of shock and numbness, the moment of hearing it is seared on the memory. Sylvia's death was a public event almost from the time that she was found.

It seems that the approach of the various arms of the State to the families of murder victims is at best haphazard and clumsy. At worst it can add to the injury already suffered.

Stella's grief was not helped by a public fascination with the murders and their victims. The murders, with all of their shocking details, were a talking point.

In the summer of 1997, four months into the murder investigation, word reached gardaí that a young heroin addict had been talking about the murders. Dean Lyons was a twenty-four-year-old homeless heroin user who regularly slept in the Salvation Army hostel in the grounds of the old St Brendan's building. The hostel, a cavernous former recreation hall divided roughly into dorms, was a place where men could get a bed, if they had the £3 and, in theory, if they had not been barred for fighting or using drugs or alcohol. By the time Dean Lyons arrived on the scene, however, the older homeless men had abandoned it to a population of mainly young drug users.

Set in a derelict field beside the old granite St Brendan's building, the walk to the door of the hostel at night was a dangerous, unlit stumble down a rubbish-strewn path. Dean was well known around the north-inner-city area, a young vulnerable man with a chronic heroin habit and a penchant for making up stories. He had shared one of those stories with a fellow addict, who went to the gardaí with his nugget of information.

Back in March of that year, Dean Lyons had watched all the commotion outside Orchard View as he wandered the streets and, as a way of drawing attention to himself, he started to spin some tales.

Gardaí had no other leads on the identity of the murderer. On the morning of Saturday, 26 July, they surrounded the Grangegorman hostel and burst in, taking Dean Lyons to the Bridewell Garda Station for questioning.

What happened in the interview room of the Bridewell during those hours of partially video-taped questioning became the subject of a high-level garda internal inquiry that has never been published. The investigating gardaí produced a statement signed by Dean Lyons, confessing to the murders.

At a special Sunday sitting of the District Court the next day, gardaí charged Dean Lyons with Mary Callinan's murder. Dressed in jumper and jeans and with his right arm in plaster, Dean was remanded in custody to appear the following day. The court was told that when he was charged in the station Dean had nothing to say.

Stella followed the developments in the case through the newspapers. A man who had lived close to where she was living was now charged with murdering her sister.

Twenty-three days after Dean Lyons stood in the dock at the Dublin District Court, there was another shocking double murder. The two victims were Carl and Catherine Doyle, a young Dublin couple in their twenties. They had moved to Carane, near Ballintubber in County Roscommon, under a rural resettlement scheme to create a new life for their four children.

On a the night of Friday, 15 August 1997, at the old farmhouse called Cnoc na Sí Óige, or the hill of the fairies, the two were stabbed to death by the boyfriend of Catherine's sister

Sarah Jane Doyle. Mark Nash stabbed Carl Doyle as he slept in an armchair before beating Sarah Jane and her sister with a stove handle and then stabbing Catherine. Sarah Jane survived the attack.

Nash went on the run and was arrested after being spotted cycling a bike at Twomileditch in Galway the following evening. He was charged with the double murder and remanded to prison.

Stella was dimly aware of the second double murder. Still in the depths of grief for her sister, she saw no connection. On the face of it there was no link between the murders in the depths of the Roscommon countryside and those in north inner city Dublin, other than the fact that all four victims had been stabbed several times in a violent frenzy.

But exactly a week after the Roscommon murders, an article in the *Irish Times* by the paper's security correspondent Jim Cusack provided another shocking development in the case. 'Second man confesses to two Grangegorman killings,' read the headline. The article could not name Mark Nash because he still faced a jury for the murders of Carl and Catherine Doyle. But the confession meant that the Grangegorman investigation was in utter disarray.

Nash had told gardaí in Galway when he was arrested that he had killed Sylvia Sheils and Mary Callinan. He gave them details that only someone who had seen the murder scene could have known.

It was a mess. The gardaí had two double murders and two apparent confessions to one of them. Nash's confession meant that Dean Lyons was an innocent man charged with murder. An internal inquiry was ordered into how the statement from the young heroin addict could have contained information that only those familiar with the layout of Orchard View could have known. It would be a further seven months before the DPP finally withdrew the charges against Dean Lyons and Lyons was released from Mountjoy prison. He moved to Britain soon afterwards.

The results of the internal inquiry by Assistant Commissioner Jim McHugh have never been made public. Nash subsequently withdrew his admissions and has never been charged with the Grangegorman murders.

Stella believes what happened to the only man to be charged with her sister's murder is as much a tragedy as Sylvia's death. His family home in Tallaght is close to her own house. In the scheme of things, both Sylvia Sheils and Dean Lyons were marginalised outsiders. If a middle-class young man had been wrongly charged with murder on the strength of a Garda statement there would have been much more outrage.

Like the rest of the country, she followed developments through the newspapers and it was in a report in the *Irish Times* that she read about Dean Lyons' death, from a heroin overdose, in a British prison in September 2000. He died aged twenty-seven.

Jim McHugh was a very nice, refined man, and he sat in Stella's living room one evening talking to her about Sylvia's death and the Grangegorman debacle. One of the country's most senior gardaí, he was known for his diplomatic handling of difficult situations. He could not tell her anything, he told her apologetically. She would have to write to the DPP.

So she wrote a number of times to the most secretive office in the civil service. She asked the DPP's office why Mark Nash had not been charged with her sister's murder. They wrote back to say they could not give her any explanation. McHugh had investigated his garda colleagues' handling of Dean Lyons. Neither Stella nor the Lyons family have had any answers to their questions.

More than five years after Sylvia's death, Stella and her solicitor Michael Finucane went to the Coroner's Court, hoping some of their questions might be answered. The long-adjourned inquest into the double murders heard that Mark Nash could not be compelled to attend. He was refusing to do so voluntarily.

The inquest was a harrowing ordeal. Stella left the courtroom as Professor John Harbison read his post-mortem report on the deaths of the two women. The clinical details were too difficult for her to hear read in open court.

Stella wanted the jury at the Coroner's Court to attach a rider to their verdict, calling for a full investigation into the circumstances of her sister's murder. The jury was advised that this was not within their powers and returned the standard verdict of 'unlawful killing'. Stella saw the inquest as an embarrassing loose end for the State she and her sister had served. The authorities would be much happier had the Grangegorman file never existed, she believes.

Stella's memories of Sylvia are not all sweetness and light. Her sister had a selfish streak, but she forgives her that. As the youngest child, Sylvia never learned to share with the next sibling up.

As she herself retired and Sylvia seemed to be 'coming out of her cloud', Stella had looked forward to spending more time with her sister. Stella's children were grown up and no matter how close her friends were, they could never be as close as 'my sister with the beautiful blue eyes'. Sylvia had their father's eyes – electric blue and unflinching.

It hurts Stella to look at pictures. There are whole books of photographs that she never looks at.

She was offered counselling, but turned it down. She was one of the only people whose stories are told here to have been offered counselling by the State. This was because she was working as a civil servant, in the Department of Agriculture, at the time of the murders. The counselling was offered as part of a workplace programme. As far as she was concerned, however, there was nothing anyone could do to relieve her pain: 'It's not that kind of pain. You just live through it and you live out of it, then maybe you're wiser. Maybe I could go it alone to the end of the world because of it.'

Vengeance does not come into her thinking about her sister's murder. 'It's just that there's a wrong done; justice doesn't prevail. There's no justice for Sylvia and none for me, because nobody has been apprehended for this dreadful deed.

'I don't really care who did it. I just feel sorry for them. I forgive them entirely. Forgiveness? Give it to them. I pity them from the bottom of my heart but I really miss my sister. We had our good times – we shared a life.'

If there was one thing the authorities could do to help the families of murder victims, Stella says, it would be to remember the humanity of the situation when they are dealing with relatives in the wake of a murder. Stella should never have heard about her sister's murder on a news report, even though Sylvia was not named in the report. If someone could have just picked up the telephone and told her, 'We're terribly sorry, but a dreadful thing has happened ...' that would have been some comfort.

Mark Nash is serving a double life sentence in Arbour Hill Prison in north Dublin for the murders of Carl and Catherine

Doyle. Shortly after his conviction he applied for a prison transfer to a British jail to serve the remainder of that sentence. This was refused by the Minister for Justice.

During judicial review proceedings taken by Nash against that decision in March 2002, the High Court heard that Nash's solicitors had been told that he 'was and remained a suspect' in the murders of Mary Callinan and Sylvia Sheils.

In February 2004 solicitor Michael Finucane wrote to Justice Minister Michael McDowell asking for an independent inquiry into the case. His letter identified five areas in which he said the Garda inquiry into the Grangegorman murders was not up to the standard required under the European Convention on Human Rights.

At the time of writing, the Minister is reported to have consulted with the Attorney General and the Garda authorities about the request for a public inquiry, and was said to be preparing to respond to the request. Stella is still waiting for answers.

Chapter 7

Death on the Curragh

In the half-world between sleep and waking, Ray Quinn surfaced with a start. 'Nightmare, nightmare, nightmare,' he thought as frantic moments flashed through his head – the sob in the dark when David found the car; the torchlight searches; the senior garda with tears in his eyes and the dreaded news.

As he became aware of his surroundings, he felt her lying next to him. A wave of relief hit him – it was just a horrible dream. He reached out to touch his wife's face. Instead of the familiar contours he felt a different shape – short hair and a wet face. It was David, his teenage son. The boy had crawled into the bed beside his dad while he slept and cried himself to sleep.

Sleep was a blessing and a curse. Every waking brought a new remembering, and a new loss. In the middle of this cold January night the shock of that loss hit him like a train. Ray Quinn felt on the brink of madness. The nightmare was reality. His wife Joyce was dead and nothing would ever be the same again.

Just two days earlier, he had pointed the video camera that she had bought him as a present at her as she sat down to poke the fire, warming herself after returning from her village shop. 'Switch that off,' she said to him, only half-annoyed. 'Those things are very intrusive.'

Joyce Quinn was murdered in January 1996 by Kenneth O'Reilly, a young local man to whom she gave a lift for what should have been a short drive across the Curragh plains on a bitterly cold night.

She had closed her small newsagent's shop in the village of Milltown as usual on that Tuesday evening, and started on the drive to the family home at Mooretown on the outskirts of Kildare. After getting into the car and forcing her off the road, O'Reilly stabbed her to death and dumped her body under gorse bushes, raping her as she lay dead or dying.

From that moment, ordinary everyday moments took on a whole new resonance. The casual video footage of her beside her fireside was the last time she would be alive on film.

Three months after her death, Ray found a notebook showing shop credit given to the O'Reillys by his wife. Three men's names appeared in the notebook, with details on the exact value of goods she had given them on credit. The most frequent name was Kenneth O'Reilly.

The last entry was on 23 January, the day of her murder. It showed that Joyce had given credit earlier that day in the sum of £18.46 to someone in the O'Reilly family. No name was written beside the entry in her neat handwriting. It was a task she had probably meant to catch up on later that night. The chances are good that the name would have been Kenneth O'Reilly. The dark-haired, ordinary-looking young man had been seen hanging around outside the shop that day, watching and waiting. The last time he was named in the little notebook as buying something on tick was on 10 January, less than two weeks before the murder.

The military life at the heart of the flat Curragh plains and the town of Kildare was in Joyce's blood. At the age of five she had come to live in the town for a time while her father, Commandant Tommy Wickham, was stationed there.

She was more than aware of the hazards of an army posting. Commandant Wickham was killed while on UN peacekeeping duty in the Golan Heights during the Arab-Israeli war in June 1967. She was just fifteen, a boarder studying for her Inter Cert at the Dominican school in Cabra. Her brother Brian, who was an army cadet, went down to the school to break the awful news to her.

Less than six years after Joyce's father died, she would marry an army man. Ray had joined the army from school as a cadet and had reached the rank of commandant, the same rank as her father, by the time she was murdered.

Joyce was the second child, a special, unexpected baby. Her mother Pat had believed she would only have the one child. They named her Joyce, as a celebration, short for 'rejoice'. When Pat Wickham walked into the house in Kildare forty-four years later to learn that her daughter was dead, she was heartbroken. 'Not Joyce. Not like this. Two violent deaths in the family,' she said. 'What did I do?'

As a boy, Ray had lived around the corner from the Wickham family as they grew up on the Navan Road in Dublin. His father was a shopkeeper and the family lived over the business, a small supermarket at Ashtown Grove. Ray knew Joyce, the pretty, blonde teenager, to see. Joyce was very much the girl-next-door. She was in his sister Ann's class at school, and they would give her a lift home if it was raining.

Although her face was familiar, it was not until the night she appeared at a cadet dance that he really looked at her.

He remembers Joyce's outfit that night vividly. It was a minidress with a high ruffled collar, like a clown's. The dress was

Ray helped out behind the counter in the very early days, but by the time Joyce died he had very little to do with the business – he did not even know how to work the cash register.

Time passed after Joyce had opened her shop, and the children grew. Nicole celebrated her twenty-first birthday, the same age Joyce was when she married Ray. David and Lisa were teenagers with the busy schedules that go with teenage lives.

On Christmas Day 1995 the Quinn family was at the Navan Road, gathering as they did every Christmas for a noisy, cheerful get-together at their grandmother Pat Wickham's house. The Quinns would always stay a few days at Joyce's old family home as other Dublin-based family members came and went from the festivities. They slept on settees, spare beds and wherever they would fit in the house.

Ray's video camera caught footage of Joyce smiling and happy at the dinner table, enjoying a rest from the shop in the home where she grew up. The camera had been a present from Joyce to Ray so that he could record life in the Lebanon.

He had often told her about the football matches in the Lebanon between the Irish soldiers and the Ghanaian peacekeepers. The African side would have their witch doctor perform a ritual on the makeshift pitch before the kick-about began, watched solemnly by both teams and spectators on the sidelines. At the airport as he was leaving for the Lebanon, she had presented him with the camera, with a grin. 'There, bring me back the pictures.'

That Christmas Ray bought Joyce a mobile phone. He had walked into Clery's on O'Connell Street the week before Christmas week and bought the Ericsson mobile with a black leather case. When he got it home he programmed in a few

as 1960s as Twiggy. She gave Ray a shy smile and a wave. Until that moment she was just some girl, a friend of his sister's, that he had set up as a dance date for his army cadet friend.

Ray decided there and then that she would be going to the next dance with him. They started going out together. He was nineteen and she was seventeen. A photographer was there to capture their first formal dance with a black-and-white portrait in the cadet's mess in the Curragh Camp. She beamed at the camera in a beaded full-length dress, her blonde hair shining, the ends flicked out, on the arm of her lanky young cadet.

After leaving school Joyce worked in the Bankers' Institute on Nassau Street in Dublin, and then with the Irish Blood Transfusion Service for just over three years. Just after her twenty-first birthday in 1973 a family friend, Father Frank O'Shaughnessy, married them in a church in Dublin's Liberties. The newly-weds lived at Frenchfurze Grove in Kildare town until Ray's job took him to a British training camp at Larkhill, near Salisbury, for a year.

They moved into married quarters and Joyce kept the gardens beautifully and looked after their toddler daughter Nicole, who had been born in 1974. During their time in England, Joyce was diagnosed with a minor gynaecological problem, which seemed to mean that Nicole would be their only child.

But, just as her own mother had had Joyce against the predictions of the doctors, Joyce's beloved David was a much-welcomed addition to the family in January 1980.

Arriving at the hospital, Ray found her sitting up in bed. She had a habit of raising her finger in the air to emphasise a point and that day she pointed at the baby. 'Come and see your baby,' she said proudly. Later, holding the boy, she told him:

'You'll never know how much I wanted this little baby.' In 1981 she got her wish again and their youngest daughter Lisa was born.

That year Ray was posted to Lebanon, and Joyce and the children moved over to live in northern Israel for three months. There followed another spell back home in Kildare, when the family moved to Mooretown, an area on the outskirts of the town, into a comfortable home and a garden that Joyce would very much make her own.

In the summer of 1988 they moved again to the Middle East. At first they lived in the Irish base at Tiberius on the Golan Heights, then in Bethlehem and for a time in Damascus.

Just like at home, there was a lively military social scene on the foreign posting. Among the other army wives Joyce chatted about work and children. But Ray felt that it was beginning to get under her skin that the other women had jobs and interests outside of their families. That, along with the fact that the three children were all at school, made Joyce decide on a new project when they returned home.

Milltown Stores had originally been a pub in the small village on the outskirts of Newbridge. The small, pitched-roof building was next to a car park for the Milltown Inn and opposite St Brigid's national school – a perfect spot for selling sweets, newspapers and basic provisions.

The shop was for sale for £44,000 in 1991. The Quinns took out a bank loan for £30,000 and used savings for the rest. For the family it meant a bit of adjusting. Joyce would open The Store, as she called her new venture, from eight in the morning until seven at night.

She was one of life's organised people. With the minimum of fuss she got her three children to school and work, ran the small shop and kept her customers happy. It was only after her death that Ray realised how much she had done around the house. Shirts did not iron themselves and meals did not just appear.

After her death, one customer remarked on how much of a friend she had been to the villagers. If a smoker customer came along as she was locking up, she would give them a packet of fags that they could pay for later. A dozen children all clamouring for a different selection of penny sweets were each dealt with patiently and with good humour.

Her routine meant something of a clockwork life, with everything coordinated around trains, school buses and the opening times of her shop. Her reliability was the thing that alerted Ray that something was wrong when she did not arrive home as planned on the night of the murder.

In their marriage, Ray was the unreliable one. One time he spent a week on a diving trip with the army divers, and they remained on in Clare after the bad weather broke and the sun came out. He had telephoned the house to say he would be away for another two days, but Joyce did not get the message. When he arrived home four days later than he should have, she joked that had he been missing another day she probably would have phoned the police. 'But then you would have turned up like a bad penny.'

Joyce was the lynchpin of the family. Only after she was gone did Ray realise how much she did, quietly and without a fuss, to keep family life ticking over.

Her business skills were also sharp. Some time after taking out the bank loan she transferred the balance to a Credit Union loan and paid off the bank. The repayments went down and the books of the village shop began to look more healthy.

numbers – the local Garda station in Kildare, the home number at Mooretown, his office number and her mother's number. He had been struck by her vulnerability after she had driven into a pothole on her way into Dublin shortly before Christmas.

Joyce had punctured two tyres on her black Citroen on a lonely stretch of the Naas Road a few weeks earlier, and had had to go to a nearby cottage for help. Afterwards Ray worried at the idea of her on her own on the side of the road, so the mobile phone was more than just a luxury.

It was not too surprising that the senior army officer was security conscious. Ray was based at Army Headquarters, on Infirmary Road on Dublin's northside, as a staff officer in the Directorate of Operations. His job was to coordinate Defence Force and Garda joint operations. If there was a search, a serious crime or terrorism operation, he would liaise with his Garda counterpart Chief Superintendent Tom King and get the Defence Forces personnel mobilised. It was a skill he never dreamed he would have to use to search for his own missing wife.

Tuesday, 23 January, began like any normal, busy day. The country woke to speculation on the airwaves about the price of beer and cigarettes as finance minister Ruairi Quinn prepared to read the Budget speech in the Dáil that day.

Joyce got up on that dark, cold morning and dressed in leggings and a long grey jumper. As the rest of the family slept she would normally drive Nicole the short distance to Kildare railway station for her 7.15am train to Dublin. That morning there was no trip to the station, as Nicole had stayed overnight in Dublin. She woke David and Lisa at 7.30am as usual. Twenty minutes later Ray left to drive to work.

After a quick breakfast, Joyce drove her two teenage children to Milltown. On the short car journey she asked David to look after the shop the following evening as she wanted to get away for a short while to drive Lisa home from Kildare. She was not happy with the thought of her daughter walking in the dark from the town to the house. No-one was to know that it was her own safety that would be at risk a few hours later.

They got to Milltown and the two children got the local bus shortly after 8.20am. They said goodbye to their mam and she spent the day working in the shop as usual. She would usually smile and wave at them through the shop window just as the bus pulled out. After her death one of the teenagers on the school bus would leave a bunch of flowers and a message addressed to Joyce, whom the child knew only as the smiling woman who waved her kids off every morning.

After school, at around 4.45pm, the two teenagers arrived back in the village. Joyce drove David home, stopping off in Kildare to pay her mobile phone bill at the post office. David went to a few shops looking for a Tippex pen that he wanted for school.

When they got home he changed and lit the fire and his mother put a dinner of pork and potatoes into the oven for roasting, telling her son to keep an eye on it and turn it down at a certain time.

She cleaned up her kitchen and put a load of washing into the machine. At 6.00pm she drove back to the shop, where Lisa was working behind the counter. Ray had driven back to Milltown from work and sat outside the shop in his car, listening to the Budget coverage on the radio.

When Joyce arrived they chatted in the shop. It was everyday, routine stuff – instructions on what vegetables to put on

Above: *James Morgan at a family wedding in Kerry before his murder, the last photograph taken of him alive.*
Right: *Gillian Bishop on the seafront in her home town of Bray, County Wicklow.*

Left:
Jonathan Edwards.
Below: *Patrick Lawlor*
and his mother
Dolores, at her
fortieth birthday
party.

Above: *Nichola Sweeney and (right) Nichola with her baby brother Christopher*

Above: *Sylvia Sheils (back row on left) with her sister Stella (front row middle) and friends on Killiney Beach.*
Below: *Sylvia Sheils as a young woman.*

Above: *Joyce Wickham and Ray Quinn photographed before an Army dance, their first date together.*

Above: *Adrian Gallagher.*
Left: *Jock Corbally.*

Right: *Phyllis Murphy.*
Below: *Joan McCarthy with husband Charlie and their grand-daughter Gemma.*

Noel Neville

for that night's dinner. He left to collect Nicole from the 6.20pm train. Joyce followed him out to the car with a copy of the *Irish Independent* and the *Evening Herald* and cartons of cigarettes that were always taken out of the shop at night for safe keeping. It was the last time he saw her alive. He drove away towards Kildare with Lisa to pick up her older sister.

It was this moment that Kenneth O'Reilly had been waiting for. As the busy family went about their daily routine he had watched and waited, a boning knife tucked inside his jacket. He had stolen it, along with other knives, from the meat plant where he once worked.

He needed things to go to plan. He needed her to be on her own, away from the shop and the possibility that a late customer would stop her for a chat or a packet of cigarettes. He needed it to be just the two of them. Now Joyce was alone, and the school gate was open. It was time for him to stand out by the side of the road in the freezing cold, stick out his thumb and rely on her good nature to let him into her car.

* * *

'Look, there's a problem,' Ray Quinn said, panic rising in his chest. 'I've checked with the immediate family. There's no reason whatever for her not to be home. There has been no emergency in her family and otherwise she would be home.'

It was 9.45pm that night and Ray was in Kildare Garda Station talking to Garda Liam Kelly, who was on duty that night.

A hunger pang had been the first indication that Joyce was not where she should have been. Ray had gone into the study to work on assembling a panic button for Joyce's sister. Engrossed in the wires and sirens, he got lost in the job and it was only when he realised that the time had come and gone for dinner that he went into the kitchen. 'I turned off the oven,' Nicole told him, 'Mam's not home yet.'

Around 8.15pm, Ray reached for the phone and dialled his wife's new mobile phone. The voice of the Eircom messaging service told him she was out of coverage. He knew the battery was fully charged and wondered if she had broken down on the road.

There were several routes she could have taken home. Ray got into his dark grey Volvo 740 and drove each one, to see if she had been stranded somewhere in the dark. He telephoned the house from the Milltown Inn to see if she had arrived home. He tried the Cash and Carry and drove to Newbridge where the mobile blood-bank van had been. The van was gone and the Cash and Carry was closed. The shop was shuttered and in darkness. Another call to her mobile went unanswered.

Back at the house, Ray rang the gardaí. He described his wife and what she was wearing, and told them emphatically there was no chance she would have gone for a drink without phoning. That was something he might have done, but not Joyce. Not with a dinner in the oven, her three children home and the fire lit.

David jumped into his dad's car and they both went out again to look for Joyce. At Milltown the teenager went into the graveyard and shone his torch around the headstones, looking for any sign. He told his dad they should check the school yard. As Ray checked the front school yard, he heard David's sob in the darkness from the back. 'There's mam's car,' David shouted. Ray ran around the corner. The worst-case scenario was beginning to unfold. The till drawer was on the back seat, empty and sitting at an angle. The doors were closed and there was no sign of Joyce.

A short while later David found his mother's black-and-grey leather handbag in a hedge. The school yard and surrounding area were now a crime scene, her belongings evidence.

Joyce hated the cold. As they searched that night and into the early hours of the next morning, it was one of the many things going through Ray's head. Conditions on the Curragh were bleak and icy. If she was tied up somewhere she would be wretchedly cold.

At daylight on Wednesday morning a massive search began. Armed soldiers arrived. Two Aer Corps helicopters and a team of locals and gardaí were assembled. Reporters and photographers had assembled at the crossroads.

Just before 10am, searchers were organised into groups of eight, with search routes printed out. An Ordnance Survey map was consulted, propped against the back windscreen of a car. Ray and David arrived at the village. David was frantic and white-faced. His father looked haggard. Both had mud on their wellington boots.

One of the helicopters was circling over fields when word came that a body had been found. In the end it was Joyce's neighbour Fergal O'Regan who found her. Along with Pat Mackey, another local man, he had gone to search an area beside the nine-hole Cill Dara Golf Club. They followed fresh car tracks on the short grass and saw Joyce lying half under a gorse bush. They phoned 999 as soon as they found her body.

Outside the Quinn house a short time later, Chief Superintendent Sean Feely had a horrible duty to perform. He knocked and waited.

'Can I see you on your own,' he said to Ray. In the lounge the garda had tears in his eyes. He had known Joyce from

Christmas dinners where gardaí and army personnel would meet. 'We found a body – out near the golf course.'

Ray was confused by the location, thinking of another golf course. 'Is there any chance it's not her? Could it be someone else?'

'No, Ray, it's Joyce,' the Chief said quietly. 'I think it was a knife.'

Seven days later, Ray Quinn walked into the Four Courts to hear Kenneth O'Reilly being charged with Joyce's murder. He had never met the young man who had been arrested and questioned after the killing. O'Reilly had lived all his life in Milltown village. He had been just seventeen when Joyce opened her shop and like the rest of the village he became a regular customer. The initial suspicion that she had been killed by someone she knew had proved correct.

As Ray leaned to the left to put down his coat in the packed courtroom, there beside him was the man who had killed his wife, head down and handcuffed. When Ray's brother Tommy was called to the stand to give evidence that he had identified Joyce's body, he had to squeeze past O'Reilly as he walked to the stand.

The idea of murder was one thing. The reality of Joyce's killer standing close enough that Ray could hear him breathing was another. O'Reilly never looked him in the eye, keeping his head down throughout the brief hearing until he was led away to be returned to Mountoy Prison.

A kind of half-life continued. The Quinn family existed in a bubble of shock. Ray would find himself wandering round the kitchen looking for the house keys. After a while he would look down to see an empty milk carton in his hand and the bunch of keys in the bin. When he looks back on it now, he is not sure he should even have been driving a car in his state.

Some time later, David went to his first dress dance, without his mum to send him off proudly with photographs at the house and a last tweak of his tie. The following morning gardaí called to the house and he had to get out of bed to look at a knife they had brought with them. They needed his evidence that he had never seen the knife before, in case O'Reilly claimed that it was Joyce's knife and he had killed her in self-defence.

It would have been a grim task for anyone. David looked at the strange boning knife in horror and confirmed that he had never set eyes on it before.

The army agreed to a transfer to Kildare for Ray, so that he could be close to home to try and manage the house and shop. At first the three children insisted that they did not want a housekeeper. No-one would replace Joyce. They told their father that everyone would do their bit. But that inevitably slipped.

Ray would return to an overflowing sink, a full dishwasher and clothes stuffed into the washing machine. Everyone would be given their jobs, but at times marshalling the troops in the barracks was a lot easier than issuing orders to his teenage children.

Meanwhile the wheels of the criminal justice system slowly began to turn. By the end of May the book of evidence was ready and had been signed for by the Chief State Solicitor's office. In December, as the Quinns faced their first Christmas without Joyce, Kenneth O'Reilly was arraigned. His barrister, Senior Counsel Paddy McEntee, told the court he would be seeking an early trial as O'Reilly was in custody. Ray was worried that he could be released on bail by the court. Lisa in particular was terrified at seeing O'Reilly again. She had been serving in the shop hours before he attacked and killed her mother. Ray had made plans to move his daughter away had O'Reilly been released.

As it turned out, O'Reilly remained behind bars and the family prepared for a trial in the spring. In February the case was listed for hearing in June. The following month the defence said they might not be ready to proceed, and the case was taken off the list. It was down for mention in May. In the end it was twenty months before the murder trial opened.

The Quinn family's long wait was not unusual. The average waiting time for a murder case to go to trial is now around twelve months. In 1996 it was twice that. The family of a murder victim could expect the anniversary of their death to come and go twice before the criminal trial was finished.

Murder cases are tried in the Central Criminal Court, effectively the High Court of the criminal courts system, usually based in the Four Courts in Dublin. However, the same court also hears all serious sexual assault cases, a situation that some judges have criticised as leading to over-long waiting times for murder cases to come to trial.

In the summer of 2003, a committee chaired by Supreme Court Judge Nial Fennelly recommended that all rape and murder cases should start in circuit courts around the country. It would then be up to the circuit court judge to decide whether a case would be heard locally, transferred to another court or brought before the Central Criminal Court. The recommendation was awaiting implementation by the end of 2003. It could, according to the Courts Service, virtually eliminate the twelve-month wait for murder cases to come to trial.

Monday, 5 October 1997, was Lisa's sixteenth birthday. It

was another family milestone coloured by Joyce's absence. A birthday cake was arranged in between efforts to discover whether O'Reilly would be pleading guilty. His trial was due to start the next day.

Ray had prepared his children to hear the evidence of their mother's murder. He had told them that the gardaí believed she was probably dead or dying when O'Reilly raped her. He wanted the court to hear how premeditated the murder had been, with O'Reilly planning his escape through the school yard even before he got into her car.

O'Reilly stood in the Central Criminal Court dressed in an Aran jumper and jeans. The young man uttered one word during the twenty-minute hearing: 'Guilty.' The Quinns were doubly relieved. A guilty plea not only meant no risk that the jury would acquit, but also meant there would be no appeal. There was legal argument over whether the court could hear a brief outline of his crime. Then, in one of his last cases before he would go on to chair the Flood Tribunal, Justice Feargus Flood sentenced O'Reilly to the mandatory sentence for murder – life in prison. Finally it was at an end.

The stuff of loss carried on long after O'Reilly started his life sentence. Ray Quinn pulled the flower bulbs out of their beds when he saw them coming up in the spring after Joyce's death. He couldn't bear to see the flowers she had planted coming back to life.

Some years later he was tidying out the attic and found some keepsakes that Joyce had carefully put away. There was a drawing of the family by Lisa. She had drawn her father with his big army boots on, and Joyce with curlers in her hair and two paw marks on her dress from the beloved family red setter Bran.

Then there were the small white envelopes he found in the attic years after she was gone, grown slightly yellow with age. Inside each was a silken lock of baby hair, one for each child. Now that Joyce was gone though, there was no-one to say which envelope belonged to which of the three children. David's was obvious with its ginger hue, but which of the two girls owned which would always be a mystery.

In May 2003 Ray became a grandfather when Nicole gave birth to her son Cian. During the pregnancy she had missed having her mother around to talk to about the impending birth. As at every family gathering since her death, Joyce was a glaring absence at the christening. Just like her mother, Nicole is devoted to her lovely new son.

A year after Joyce's murder, Ray wrote to the women TDs in the Dáil. He pointed out that nineteen women, including his wife, had died violently in 1996, and appealed to them as women to lobby for key changes in the criminal justice system.

The first would be a change in the law to oblige suspects to provide DNA samples; the second was representation in the courts for the families of murder victims. He also insisted that a better state pathology service was needed; and that the lay-out of the courts should be improved to avoid the awful situation where victims' families rub shoulders with their loved ones' killers.

Six years later, the move to make taking a DNA sample easier has been put in train, with a bill to reclassify saliva as a non-intimate sample which therefore can be taken without a suspect's consent. Human rights organisations have criticised the measure and said it could lead to the abuse of prisoners in Garda stations.

Legal representation for victims has still not been addressed in any meaningful way. Rape victims are entitled to be represented by a barrister in court, but only if their own sexual history is under examination by the court. The state pathology service is still understaffed following the retirement of Dr John Harbison, and changes to the majority of the country's ageing courtrooms are a long way off.

'Effecting these changes will not impact on my family's circumstances, but we would like to feel that out of the trauma and devastation that has been inflicted on us, some good could come,' Ray wrote in February 1997.

The Store at Milltown has been renamed by its new owner. On a busy summer morning it is still a hub of activity, a central point for the tiny village of fifty houses. David and his dad have put in a rock pool in the back garden, stocked with glittering fish. Now they will put a safety mesh over it so that Cian can play there safely. Joyce would have been proud.

Chapter 8

I'll not be long

It was small talk between strangers in Dún Laoghaire Town Hall that afternoon. Michael Gallagher had walked to one side of the large room with his cup of tea and hot sausage roll. A few minutes later a couple and their daughter happened to sit beside him. They didn't know him and he didn't know them. They chatted pleasantly. The woman said she remembered the hall when it had been a dance hall; she used to dance there when she was young.

There were a lot of people in the room that day. Maybe it was coincidence, or maybe a kind of gravitational pull, but later, when the Lord Mayor asked Michael if he wanted to meet the family of a victim of the Dublin-Monaghan bombings, the white-haired Donegal man found himself being introduced to the Masseys, the couple with whom he had just shared his tea break.

Frank Massey and his wife Annie lost their twenty-one-year-old daughter Anna in May 1974. That afternoon in October 1998 was just weeks after Michael's twenty-one-year-old son Adrian smiled at him from the doorway, saying, 'I'll not be long,' and went to his death in the Omagh bombing.

Both sets of parents had lost children who had just come of age – Anna and Adrian, obliterated by acts of terrorism just as their adult lives were beginning. A friendship was formed.

Now each father phones the other on the anniversary of their child's death.

Michael had travelled to Dún Laoghaire with Marion Radford, whose fifteen-year-old son Alan also died in the Omagh bomb. A tree was planted in the People's Park for the twenty-nine people who were killed that sunny Saturday afternoon on Omagh's Lower Market Street. A second tree was planted for the victims of the Dublin-Monaghan bombings twenty-four years earlier.

More than five years have passed since Michael Gallagher and his wife Patsy lost their only son. That tree-planting was one of the first of many formal occasions that Michael would attend as chairman of the Omagh Support and Self-Help Group. Adrian's death has transformed his father's life from car mechanic to campaigner. His working hands have been shaken by those of the world's most powerful people: Tony Blair, Bill Clinton and the Queen of England. But his faith in the establishment represented by those powerful people has been severely tested. He says he would gladly swap all his encounters with heads of state for one handshake with his son.

In the years since Adrian's death Michael has grown wary of politics and spin. Now he looks back on those early days as hopelessly naive times, when the massive outpouring of sympathy and goodwill made the people of Omagh believe that their catastrophe would change things.

Michael tried to move on after 15 August 1998, to put it behind him and go back to his garage business, but he was constantly looking over his shoulder and thinking all the time about what he should be doing about the bombing and its aftermath.

It was up to the victims, he believed, to show leadership – a leadership that politicians could not provide, because they could not truly understand the effects of terrorism. As a family the Gallaghers have had more reasons to understand the shocking impact of terrorist atrocities than most.

Michael was the eldest of eleven children from a Donegal family. He was brought up in St Johnston, a small border village just four miles from Derry city, until the age of nine, when the family moved to Glasgow.

In 1968 his parents brought their family home and moved to Omagh, where for the first time the teenage Michael saw policemen carrying pistols. The image was startling, a sign that in this new town normal life was different.

Glasgow had been a sectarian city, but the hatred was compressed into Saturday afternoons when Celtic played Rangers and the city divided along tribal lines. Come Monday morning when Glaswegians returned to work, the animosity was shelved for another week.

The year of the Gallagher family's move to Northern Ireland marked the start of the Troubles. It was a dangerous time to be a young man in the North, a time when you could be shot for your religion if you were in the wrong place at the wrong time.

Omagh enjoyed a sort of innocence as violence took a grip in Belfast and Derry. As a garrison town, like Athlone, the tension between troops and locals was eased by a kind of integration. The town could be friendly and close.

In those relatively innocent days, soldiers mixed with local families, married Omagh girls and became part of the fabric of the town when they left the army and took up jobs as postmen, barmen and taxi drivers.

Just as his son would grow to live and breathe cars, Michael was a car-mad young man, and one of his friends, Sean O'Connor, shared a garage with his father. Sitting in the garage was a shiny red Mini. When Michael asked his friend who owned it Sean told him, 'That's Patsy's.' Michael knew another man called Patsy Flynn and assumed the Mini-owner was male. It wasn't until Sean's sister Patsy came home from her nursing job in Kent that he realised the owner of the smart red Mini was a Patricia and not a Patrick.

The fancy he had taken to her car transferred to the young nurse and Michael and Patsy started going out together. They were married in 1973 and moved into a small house at Wood-side Terrace in the town.

Three weeks before Christmas that year the Provisional IRA detonated a 600lb van bomb outside the RUC station beside the terrace. The row of houses was decimated and the young couple were never able to return to their first home. They went to live in the Hospital Road area, a traditionally Protestant part of Omagh. Their next-door neighbours were another couple, Stanley and Ann McCombe. It was to be another cruel irony in the many strands that linked the victims of the Omagh bomb. Twenty-five years later, Ann would die in the bomb along with Adrian Gallagher.

Life in Omagh was relatively peaceful for the Gallaghers until June 1984, when a provisional IRA murder squad ambushed and shot dead Michael's youngest brother Hugh.

It was the night of Saturday, 3 June 1984, when Michael was working an evening shift in his taxi, that he last saw his brother alive. Hugh Gallagher had been driving another cab. The two brothers exchanged a few words through the car windows around midnight, outside Elliot's convenience store in

Omagh town centre, and Michael carried on working before going home to his bed.

At around four in the morning there was a knock at the door. It was James, another brother. 'That's a fancy nightgown,' James said to him after he had let him in the door. Confused and bleary-eyed, Michael asked him what he wanted at that hour. 'They shot Hughie,' James told him. 'Is he dead?' Michael asked. 'He is.'

James had just come from identifying the dead man on the roadside in the grey light before dawn. Hugh was found by police on a routine patrol, slumped at the wheel of his taxi on the outskirts of Omagh.

Hugh Gallagher was a target for the IRA because he had resigned six months earlier from the Ulster Defence Regiment, where he had been a part-time soldier. The West Tyrone Brigade of the provisional IRA had, with a ruthless efficiency, carried out more than a dozen such murders, targeting Catholics who worked for the security forces. They ambushed the twenty-six-year-old and shot him dead as a savage message to others.

Hugh was a father of two children – Heather, who was five at the time, and Paul, who was three. Michael's children remembered him as their young and vibrant Uncle Hughie. Once, during a family trip to Enniskillen swimming pool, Hugh had spotted his little nephew Adrian go under the surface of the water. The boy was swimming behind his father and Michael had not seen the problem. Hugh reacted quickly, grabbing the boy under the water and bringing him up gulping air and coughing water. Adrian always remembered his uncle Hughie was the one who saved him. No-one could know that both rescuer and rescued would be lost at the hands of terrorists years later.

After their uncle died Michael's three children – Sharon, Adrian and Cathy – were frightened to see their father leaving for work. They would constantly ask him where he was going and when he would be back.

The taxi business turned to minibuses and wedding limousines, and along with that went the repair garage where Michael maintained the vehicles. After a while the garage started to take off, so Michael gave up the driving and took in repair jobs, working out of a garage at the family home at Loughview Cottages.

Adrian, who was always called Aidan by friends and family, was a constant presence. As a boy he loved to watch his father working, and he pottered about in the garage absorbing everything about the business of car maintenance. When he wasn't in his father's garage he was listening to music in his bedroom and seeing his friends, both Catholic and Protestant. Cars and music were his big passions. Politics were of no interest.

After leaving school Adrian went to college in Portadown, to turn his interest in cars into a profession. He qualified in light vehicle body repair and decided to stay at home to build the family business with his father. It was to be a father and son shop, the car-mad boy and his quiet dad working together.

Michael Gallagher was under a car when he heard the blast. Explosions were a familiar sound. But this blast had a different ferocity. It was a loud, lasting noise. It seemed to continue after the initial bang, the sound hanging in the air. He pushed himself out from under the car, locked up the garage and drove home. He could see a pall of smoke rising, but he could not tell the whereabouts of the bomb. He never dreamed it could have been in the busy town centre.

That morning another bomb had been on his mind as he walked through the aisles of the local supermarket with Patsy. The family had taken the previous week off to treat his grandson Dara to a week of day trips, a kind of consolation treat after a wet and fairly miserable summer. Buncrana had been the destination on the Wednesday before the bomb, and on Friday they had headed to Belfast Zoo.

He took Patsy to do the shopping on Saturday as the fridge needed to be restocked after a week of being out and about. In the supermarket a newspaper caught his eye. 'Boy in the iron mask gets wed today,' read the headline in the *Mirror*. The story was about Stephen Ross, a twenty-six-year-old man who had been horribly injured as a teenager in the Enniskillen poppy day bombing eleven years earlier.

That Saturday was Stephen Ross's wedding day. The 'iron mask' was the orthopaedic frame used to hold his facial bones together after reconstructive surgery. The photographs of his injuries shortly after the bombing showed just the boy's eyes looking out of the mask, a shocking image of the legacy of an IRA bomb.

Now Stephen Ross was to marry his fiancé at a village near Basingstoke in Hampshire. On that sunny morning, Michael thought what a good day it was for somebody to be getting their life together. At that stage it was only hours before his life and hundreds of others would change forever. With the IRA on ceasefire and the peace process in train, no-one expected to see another Enniskillen. But as Michael was struck by one victim's story the worst single bomb of the Troubles was already on its way to his home town.

He went to the garage premises after dropping Patsy home and returned at around midday for lunch. He asked where

Adrian was. 'Upstairs,' Patsy told him, changing for a trip into town. Adrian had been out that morning paying bills for paints and other materials for the business. Afterwards he planned a trip to the town centre with his close friend Michael Barrett to buy some boots and jeans.

Adrian came down to the kitchen and asked Patsy what his waist size was. She had always bought the clothes for her twenty-one-year-old, six-foot-two son. They laughed and Michael told him not to worry – the shop girls would put a measuring tape on him and tell him his size. At the last minute he turned in the kitchen doorway and smiled at his parents. 'I'll not be long,' he said.

By the time Michael got back to the house after the bomb, Patsy and their daughters Cathy and Sharon were getting anxious. The town had filled with the noise of sirens and helicopters. Cathy turned on the teletext and news flashed up of a bomb in the town centre. Up to ten people were dead, the bulletin said. Michael knew if there were ten dead then hundreds would be injured. 'Put that TV off,' he told Cathy. 'And don't turn it on again.'

Knowing the bomb scene would be sealed off by police, Michael went straight to the hospital. He arrived less than half-an-hour after the explosion, to a nightmare world of blood and terror. Dozens of people were arriving in ambulances, cars and vans. Some of the wounded had even walked the quarter-mile from the bomb site to the doors of the hospital. At the helipad he watched an ambulance reversing at speed to the door of a helicopter, as another helicopter hovered above waiting to land.

It reminded him of images he had seen of Vietnam in the 1960s, but instead of soldiers the wounded were women and children. Just two nurses and one doctor had been on duty that Saturday afternoon. A bad car crash would have been the worst they should have expected. Within half an hour more than 300 people had arrived, some of them fatally wounded.

Michael saw a woman lying dead in a corridor as he scanned the scene for signs of his son. He didn't know what he was going to see or what he was really looking for, other than a scrap of clothing, jeans or a shoe to indicate that Adrian was there. There was nothing and Michael left, thinking, 'Thank God he's not here.'

Back at home Michael Barrett's father had arrived and both men returned to the hospital to look together for their sons. Television cameras and press photographers had joined the commotion at the doors of the hospital. Michael saw a man walking towards him, his outstretched arms holding two plastic shopping bags. 'This is all I have left of my wife and son,' the man was saying. Michael didn't know him at the time, but the man was Billy Jameson and the two plastic bags contained clothing that medical staff had cut off his wife Ursula and son William when they were admitted for treatment. Both actually survived the bomb, although they were badly injured.

As Billy spoke to him, Michael suddenly felt the television cameras and photographers gather round. Although he had been relatively calm until that point, a panic gripped him and he felt a huge urge to run. 'I've got to get out of this,' he told himself. 'I've got to get away.' As the cameras honed in on the scene it was as if the reality of Omagh was starting to happen. The real became more real. This was not some daylight nightmare. History was already starting to be recorded and there was still no sign of his beloved son.

On their way back to the house a second time, Michael Gallagher drove by the car park where Adrian would normally leave Patsy's car. There were just two cars in the deserted car park. One of them was the black Rover that Adrian had driven to town. The sight of the car was like a punch in the gut. Michael found it hard to breathe and thought he might collapse. He knew then they were in trouble.

He kept the news of the car without its driver to himself when they returned home for a third time. Cathy had lit a candle and put it in the window.

On a third visit to the hospital they found Michael Barrett, badly burnt and awaiting transfer to Belfast. He told Michael that the last thing he remembered was Adrian walking beside him.

Seventeen hours would pass from the time of the bomb until Michael's search for his missing son ended in an army hangar at Lisanelly Barracks.

At Omagh Leisure Centre that evening a dreadful vigil had started. People stood shocked and silent, waiting while the lists of the injured and their locations in hospitals were posted up on walls. There was a quiet dread and a palpable sense of powerlessness.

The only certainty was that the bomb had exploded at 3.05pm that day. Now all the families could do was wait for news about what had happened to those who had been standing close to it. A Tannoy made infrequent announcements. Each time it crackled into life people stiffened with fear.

The crowds that had first gathered began to thin out as the hours went on. Families who found their loved ones on lists rushed to see them. Eventually there were three groups left:

the journalists; clergy and other community leaders and supporters; and those knots of people who would not have a hospital bed to visit.

Michael approached a policeman after yet another list without Adrian's name was posted up. 'We've heard a lot about the injured,' he said. 'Surely there must be some news about the dead.' Half-an-hour later he was called down to a side room where two police officers sat, a man and a woman. They had a printed questionnaire on the table and they noted Michael's answers. Did his son have any distinguishing marks on his body – birthmarks, scars or tattoos? What had he been wearing?

None of the questions gave Michael any hope that he was going to hear anything but the worst news.

After the questionnaire and the paperwork were matched with a body the police believed was Adrian's, Michael was taken to the makeshift mortuary. James – his brother who had identified Hughie fourteen years earlier – went with Michael.

They sat silently in a waiting area with another small group. With horror they heard that the elderly man sitting beside them was waiting for news of his wife, daughter and granddaughter. Later they heard the man's daughter had been pregnant with twins.

Afterwards they realised they had been waiting with the Grimes family, whose loss that day was unthinkable in its scale. Michael Grimes' wife Mary had been killed along with their daughter Avril Monaghan. Avril was thirty-four weeks pregnant with twin girls and had been carrying her eighteen-month-old daughter Maura on her shoulders when the blast killed them all. Three generations, including two baby girls who never got to take their first breath, blown away in an instant.

Then came their turn. Adrian was wheeled in on a mortuary trolley and it was too much for Michael. There was no way he could look at his son. James once more identified a body – first his brother and now his nephew.

Back at home, Michael's face told Patsy and the girls everything. 'Aidan'll not be coming home,' he said simply.

Much later they realised that they were one of the first families to go through the identification process, even though they had waited seventeen hours after the explosion. There were other people who waited days longer, but for whom, at the end of the process, there was very little left to identify, such was the impact of the blast on those nearest the bomb car.

Omagh was now a worldwide story. Massive press interest was part of the shock waves that emanated from the detonation of the bomb. Early on Sunday morning, there was a knock on the Gallaghers' front door. A young woman reporter from London stood on the doorstep, along with a photographer, and Michael invited them inside.

His brother James followed them into the living room, protective of the family's privacy. 'Who are these people?' he asked. 'We're from the *Daily Mirror*,' the reporter said. 'You're the people who always get it wrong,' James replied.

'What did we get wrong?' she asked. 'Well, look, it doesn't really matter,' Michael's brother answered. 'Look, I promise you this,' the reporter said. 'We'll get this right.'

Michael spoke to them about Adrian and the events of the day before. As far as he was concerned the media did go on to 'get it right' in Omagh.

Very soon the victims' families organised so that those people unable to deal with the media were protected. Those who could put themselves forward fed the daily need for stories and angles on what was now one of the biggest stories of the Troubles.

'Who better to tell the world about the sort of people that lost their lives in Omagh other than the families themselves?' was Michael Gallagher's reasoning. 'We were the people that should tell the story of Omagh, not others.'

At Adrian's funeral the Bishop of Derry, Dr Francis Lagan, stopped to shake the hand of John O'Connor, Adrian's grandfather. Michael could see in his father-in-law's face that he was thinking it should be him in the coffin and not his grandson.

The two shared a birthday. If Adrian had not been killed he would have been twenty-two on 2 October. It had always been a special birthday – a joint birthday party was usually held with two cakes. John would have been eighty-two that October, exactly sixty years older than his grandson.

Ten days after Adrian's funeral John O'Connor died. He said very little in the days between his grandson's and his own death.

With the death of Patsy's father following so soon, the two weeks turned into one long wake. Friends arriving for John's funeral were sympathising with the family over Adrian's death too. For Patsy the double loss was devastating.

After Adrian's funeral the family returned home exhausted. One by one they went upstairs to bed. Michael was the last to climb the stairs in the quiet house. As he was turning off the hall light he said aloud, 'Aidan – if you're here – never leave us.'

Michael Barrett visited the Gallaghers every day for nearly three years. He had a front door key and would sit in the kitchen talking about his friend, or just sitting quietly. The fact that he lived and Adrian died, even though they were standing almost shoulder to shoulder on the street, left him with severe survivor guilt. On his birthday, Patsy asked him what he had done that day a year earlier. 'Me and Aidan went out for a drink to the pub,' he said.

In October 1998, shortly after the funerals had ended, some of the families of the victims organised a meeting in a local hotel. There had been informal gatherings in each others' houses as a support network of those worst affected began to grow.

At the meeting Michael Gallagher was elected chairman. It was the first time he had ever done anything like that. The next day he went to the local library to get a book on the duties of a chairman.

The Omagh Support and Self-Help Group was formed to put the families centre-stage on how the aftermath of the bomb would be handled. Until then they felt that the authorities were dealing with *them* as a problem that had to be handled. The powers that be seemed to be taking charge of their lives and they wanted to regain some control. A celebrity football match organised in the weeks after the bomb saw invitations going out to the families, but arriving the day after the match had been played. It was a small insult, but an insult nonetheless. They wanted a strong voice in the politics of Omagh.

And they were serious politics. There were two huge challenges the families had to face. The first was growing disquiet over what the police, both North and South, knew in the run-up to the bombing, and how the bomb investigation was being handled. The second was the inquest – living through the clinical examination of how their loved ones had died.

The three-week inquest began at the Omagh Leisure Centre in September 2000 under the coroner John Leckey. The Courts Service had flown over a top press liaison person to deal with the huge media interest. Rules were laid down that only one journalist would be admitted to ask questions and that this interview would have to be shared.

Michael Gallagher and his old neighbour Stanley McCombe were having none of it. A marquee erected for members of the public who wanted to listen to the proceedings was not being used, as there was no demand. It became the families' space for a daily press conference, where every journalist could ask any question they liked.

As the days went on the inquest was increasingly hard on the families. A babble of police radio traffic was played on the public address system, the sound of the panic and confusion that preceded the bomb, the phone calls and tape-recorded police messages. As a result of the vagueness of the bomb warning, the Saturday afternoon shoppers were being unwittingly herded by police into the path of the bomb.

In the minds of the relatives there had always been the question of whether more could have been done to avert the catastrophe. The inquest was the final straw – they now demanded to know why the Army had not been called out that day to deal with the bomb scare.

For Michael Gallagher the inquest also raised an agonising doubt over whether his son had died instantly.

Since the bombing the group had held meetings with senior RUC policemen, including the then chief constable Ronnie Flanagan. No stone would be left unturned in the hunt for the bombers, they were assured.

Then, in July 2001, the *Sunday People* newspaper printed a story headlined 'I told cops about Omagh'. The allegations, from a British security force agent known as Kevin Fulton, raised serious questions about the police handling of intelligence in the lead-up to the atrocity.

The police ombudsman Nuala O'Loan undertook an investigation, and reported her findings in December that year. She stated that Fulton had had five key meetings with his police handler between June and August 1998, during which he had passed on information about dissident republican activities. Two of the contact sheets outlining these meetings had gone missing from RUC Special Branch records. O'Loan also outlined an anonymous warning call received eleven days before the bomb, stating that the police in Omagh would come under a terrorist attack. She concluded that even if reasonable action had been taken, it was 'unlikely the Omagh bomb could have been prevented'. She said, however, that the victims and their families had been 'let down by defective leadership, poor judgment and a lack of urgency.'

South of the border, questions were also raised about intelligence available to gardaí. Garda Sergeant John White, himself under investigation as part of the inquiry into allegations of corruption against gardaí in Donegal, made contact with Michael and told him of allegations that a high-level Garda informant codenamed 'Budget' had warned that dissident republicans were planning a bombing.

According to White's allegations, Budget was one of the Garda's top informants, a car thief who allowed the vehicles he stole for terrorists to be fitted with tracking devices by the Gardaí.

After many hours talking to the garda, Michael referred John White to the Police Ombudsman's office of Northern Ireland and White was interviewed by investigators. Nuala O'Loan took the report of these allegations to Dublin and delivered it to Foreign Affairs Minister Brian Cowen.

A Government-appointed committee delivered a confidential report on the Budget allegations to Justice Minister Michael McDowell in the summer of 2003. On Monday, 8 September 2003, Michael and Patsy and eight other relatives of those killed travelled to Dublin to meet the minister and ask for information on what the three-man team had uncovered. At a meeting lasting over two hours in his office at the Department of Justice on St Stephen's Green, McDowell told them he could not go into detail about the report until he had made a statement to the Dáil.

The team tasked with investigating John White's allegations was made up of civil servants: Dermot Nally, a former secretary to the Government; Eamonn Barnes, the former DPP; and Joe Brosnan, a former secretary of the Department of Justice. The truth about who exactly knew what and when has yet to be established.

Michael Gallagher has found himself in a murky world of claim and counter-claim about Special Branch and intelligence service tactics and the use of informants against terrorist organisations. He decided to pass on whatever he was told to the Ombudsman's office in Belfast, where they would be qualified to decide if the allegations were true. In the Republic no such office existed for an independent inquiry, as the slow process of setting up an office with adequate powers and independence to police the Gardaí is still unfinished.

At home in Loughview Cottages, building work has started on Adrian's dream house. He had drawn up plans for an extension to the family cottage where they had grown up. This was to be his home. The family had kept the cottage when they moved across the road in 1985.

His plans were detailed and precise. Every door was hung to open in a certain direction to maximise space. Patsy worked closely with him and knew all his plans, down to the colour of the cooker and the type of bathroom suite he was planning to install.

The Gallaghers are carrying out Adrian's plans to the letter and will move to that house to live there. Across the road in their present home, the curtains in Adrian's bedroom have never been opened. His clothes, music, shoes, books and belongings are all where he left them more than five years ago.

The only time Adrian's door is opened is when Christmas presents or Easter eggs for the grandchildren are being hidden.

There will be a process of letting go when the move to the newly renovated house happens. Michael remembers packing up the contents of his parents' garage some years after Hugh's death. He found a wind chime that had belonged to his brother – a simple mobile of riders on horseback. 'Just leave it there,' his father said as the rest of the stuff was packed for the move. It was his father's way of moving on. And when Patsy and Michael move to the new house they will also decide to let go of some of Adrian's things.

The new house will have a room for the things they keep. It is the room where Dara, the Gallagher's grandson, will sleep when he visits, so it will be a living space for a growing boy rather than a frozen memorial to their dead son.

A brand new pair of steel-toed boots, that Adrian bought just before he died, will always be in the room. He had walked to Taggarts, a shop in Omagh near the chapel, and bought the work boots before his trip to Lower Market Street. Instead of carrying them with him while he went looking for jeans, he doubled back to the nearby car park and put them on the passenger seat of his mother's car. When he died his family found them still in car. Someone put them on top of his bed. And since then they have stayed there, unworn.

The Gallaghers talk about Adrian every day. As far as they are concerned he is still part of the family. It would be too painful not to talk about him. They laugh about him, at the things he would say, at what he would do in reaction to events that happen in the family.

Patsy feels his presence in the house. It is as if he was listening the night his father stood on the landing in the dark and pleaded with him not to leave. His death has transformed their lives. It has left a burning energy and drive to find out the truth of Omagh, a massacre of innocents on a sunny Saturday afternoon.

Chapter 9
Still searching for Jock

It was dusk now and Derek Corbally had a decision to make. Should he put his hand into the bag he had just found or wait until the following morning and come back? There was something suspicious in the dense tangle of briars and branches. But the batteries in his torch had weakened to just a watery beam and daylight was fading.

He had been in the field in Straffan, County Kildare, all day. Now, in the darkness of the ditch, it was impossible to see what it was that had been pushed deep in there. Whatever it was it was wrapped in a long plastic bag or series of bags and tied up tightly with twine.

He took a deep breath, put his hand in and felt the horrible combination of bone and flesh. There was a rush of emotion and revulsion. He turned around and threw up. He thought he had might just have found his older brother.

The gardaí arrived after a quick phone call to Detective Inspector Brian Sherry and the scene was cordoned off. Unfortunately the efforts were all for nothing. Someone had dumped the body of a large Alsation dog, wrapping the animal in bin bags before tying it up and pushing it into the ditch. Derek is still disturbed by the memory of that evening.

Since William 'Jock' Corbally disappeared in March 1996, Derek and his brothers have searched for his body and tried to piece together the method and madness of his murder. The results of their searches in the fields of Straffan have been brought in carrier bags to the Gardaí for forensic examination. Along with the dead dog there have been other animal bones and ancient human bones. At the time of writing there is still no sign of Jock.

The Corbally family moved from Summerhill in Dublin's north inner city to Finglas in 1957. Dublin Corporation was re-housing families from the hardship of inner-city life to the brave new world of Corporation estates. Finglas was country – extreme country – to any family used to living in the city. Maureen and Bill Corbally had been living over a cake shop in Summerhill with their three sons.

The house in Finglas had gardens front and back. But there were still anxieties about moving what seemed like a great distance from their roots. They had come from streets where everyone knew everyone else, but in Finglas there were new neighbours, people they did not know. They were all like splinters from the old communities as families were chosen from all over the city to start these new neighbourhoods.

Maureen walked her baby son Derek in a pram from Summerhill to the new house. The rest of the furniture and belongings went on a horse and cart.

William Corbally was her second eldest. He was a dreamer and a schemer, always trying to find new ways to make money. When he was a teenager he got a job on the Curragh riding horses. The move to that profession earned him his nickname. Although his jockey career never took off, the brief stint stayed with him as he was known for ever more as Jock.

Some of his schemes could have been sound, but without any financial footing or backing he usually fell foul of the law along the way. He started a log round, delivering firewood to heat the new homes that were springing up in what used to be the fields around them. However, instead of buying the logs he would get them by cutting down trees in the night. He was found out and that was the end of the log round. The gardaí got to know Jock and his schemes.

He was a wild kid and his best friend, PJ Judge, was an even wilder kid. The two teenage pals robbed orchards and gave cheek to the guards, kicked balls around on the streets and ran wild.

By the time Jock Corbally died he had amassed over twenty convictions. They included minor motoring offences – such as driving without tax and insurance – a post office robbery and being caught behind the wheel of a container lorry packed high with crates of Larry Goodman's beef.

He was the father of four, two from his marriage and two from a subsequent relationship. His get-rich schemes almost always got him in trouble with the law.

At least once he risked worse trouble than a prison sentence. After his death a serious criminal told his brother that Jock had sold him boxes of vodka one Christmas. The only problem was that the vodka bottles contained tap water. Jock had collected the empties at the back of a pub, and found the stash of bottle tops and the original boxes. He carefully cleaned up the bottles and filled them from the tap and then super-glued the caps back in place before packing them into the boxes. His customer was not amused at the con trick.

PJ Judge went on to a more serious and profitable life of crime. From his family home in Finglas, Judge had built up a carefully-constructed drug empire, employing heroin addicts to courier and sell his drugs, slowly and methodically amassing a fortune in drug money and a ruthless reputation.

As Jock dreamed up his Walter Mitty schemes, Judge built his reputation as a dangerous man who could not be crossed. By the early 1990s Judge had become a kingpin in the drugs trade in the north city. It was then that Judge gave a slab of cannabis to Jock's two teenage sons to sell on the streets for him. The teenagers smoked the hash, all £800 worth, and had no money to give to Judge when he came looking for it.

Judge approached Jock to settle his sons' debt. Jock told him to forget about the money, that he was not getting it. Then Judge confronted one of the boys and told him exactly what he would do to him if he did not get the money. Jock confronted his old friend and told him to lay off. It was a public shouting match and Jock squared up to Judge. Judge did not come off the better.

Jock Corbally did not know just how powerful PJ Judge had become. Building a drugs empire meant building a reputation for extreme brutality towards anyone who reneged on a debt. Drug addicts were severely beaten when they owed Judge modest amounts, earning him the nickname 'the Psycho'. It sent out the message that Judge's debts, large or small, were to be paid. Jock was warned by another brother who had heard about Judge's violence to be extremely careful. Judge was now looking for over £2,000 to be paid back. Jock's sister Sandra called to Judge's house and offered to pay him the full amount. Judge refused to take her money. It was Jock's debt and Jock had to pay it.

But another get-rich-quick idea got in the way of the growing feud, by landing Jock in prison. Jock knew when he walked into the Butterley industrial estate in Coolock in the early 1990s that the truck was probably being watched. But someone had paid him and he was going to do the job for a bit of easy money.

The container lorry had been stolen the day before and left for collection in the yard. The gardaí had found it before it was picked up and a surveillance unit was put on the container to arrest whoever came to collect. As soon as Jock Corbally climbed into the cab and went to start the lorry he was arrested. He got five years for the robbery. The sentence took him out of the path of PJ Judge for a while.

Maureen Corbally did not believe her son could do anything wrong. She could be tough with the rest of the kids, reprimanding anyone who got into trouble, but not with Jock. She hoped one day he would get a job, or that one of his ideas would turn into the money-spinner he hoped for.

For his part, her second-eldest son never really thought through his plans to their conclusion. The consequences of what he was doing, like getting behind the wheel of a watched consignment of stolen beef, were never really a reality for him.

Jock had become a real thorn in the side of PJ Judge. The drug dealer's associates gave him a hard time about the Finglas feud and the fact that his old friend had bettered him. The fury and resentment grew. At night Judge would wake up and swing a chain off the walls of Jock's house, calling his name.

Upon his release from prison, Jock would became an easy target for assassination. He lived in a small flat in Ballymun. Without a car, he walked nearly everywhere and often walked to Finglas to his mother's house. At any stage Judge could have had him shot. It would have been clean and easy simply to pay a hired killer to take his revenge and send out the message that Judge was no mug.

Jock's family believe that such an assassination would not have banished Judge's demons. He had to be personally involved in the murder of his former friend. That took planning and organisation. Judge had to put together a team of people, none of whom would know what the rest of the team was doing. His plotting would put PJ and Jock face-to-face for the last time.

The horrific death of Jock Corbally was a rubicon that PJ Judge crossed, as far as fellow criminals in the Dublin underworld were concerned. There is little in the way of nobility in the world of drug dealers. Nothing so noble as a criminal code exists. But the punishment that Judge inflicted on his archenemy was beyond reason. It was the act of a psychotic individual rather than simply a hard-nosed businessman. And if the Psycho – as Judge was known – could do that to an old friend, what could he do to a rival in the drugs business, the criminal fraternity wondered?

Afterwards it was generally agreed that a good beating was all Jock had deserved for his clash with Judge. Even the criminal who had bought the tap water thinking it was vodka agreed that what happened to Jock should never have happened.

The criminal grapevine started to whisper as soon as Jock disappeared. The revulsion about his murder meant that people talked. Underworld figures made contact with Jock's family, even though they must have been terrified that Judge would find out. The Corballys set about trying to piece together Jock's last moments.

What they discovered was that PJ Judge had lured Jock to his death slowly and carefully. The first move was a phone call from a Coolock criminal Jock knew, to say that he had a nice bit of work for him. The man offered him money to move packages around the city. Jock knew it was drugs, but it was also easy money. The offer was made, but then again and again the date for Jock to do his first job was put back. The stop-start factor was very deliberate, to make him more eager, so that when the phone call finally came there would be no hesitation on Jock's part.

Jock was in his mother's house in Finglas in March 1996 when the final reel-him-in phone call came. The voice on the phone belonged to Declan Griffin, a Coolock criminal, and Jock was told to get a taxi to Ballyfermot. Unknown to Jock, Griffin was working with PJ Judge. It would emerge years later that Griffin was also a Garda informant.

Judge's plan nearly fell at the first hurdle. Jock did not have money for the taxi fare to Ballyfermot. Neither his mother nor his sister could lend it to him. Maureen gave her son the price of ten cigarettes. Then a friend who had a car said he could give Jock a lift, not all the way to Ballyfermot, but as far as Chapelizod as the friend had a date to take his girlfriend to the pictures.

At Chapelizod, Jock rang Griffin and said he would meet him by the phone boxes. A while later Griffin drove by and picked him up. At the car park of the Red Cow hotel the two men met Mark Dwyer, another young Dublin criminal.

The men then drove out along country roads to a field in Baldonnel. In that field, waiting in another car with two associates, was PJ Judge. Over the following hours of that cold night, Jock Corbally was beaten to death by his old enemy. The story is told that Jock's teeth were smashed in the assault, partly to hinder identification of his body and partly out of sheer viciousness.

In the second car Judge and his associates drove across country with Jock's body in the boot. Somewhere in Straffan they unloaded the body, and buried it. Judge's work was done and the Corbally family's had only just started.

The search for Jock started as a mission for the benefit of Maureen Corbally. Her family wanted to return the body of her second eldest to her, to give her the opportunity to stand at his graveside and see him buried, to give her somewhere to visit when she wanted to talk to Jock.

Five years after Jock's disappearance Maureen died, succumbing to the cancer that her family believe Jock's death brought on. She never had a place to visit and in her mind she could never grasp the fact of his death. Without the rite of passage of a funeral, a putting to rest of her son, she only remembered him as he was when he was alive.

When it was raining outside she would sit and cry, imagining him getting wet in his unmarked grave. When it was cold she cried for her boy and talked about how he would be freezing.

In the absence of a body, Maureen Corbally believed at times that her son was alive. As far as she was concerned, it was as if Jock would walk up the driveway any day. It was a way of thinking that affected all the family. Even with all the knowledge that he gathered about his brother's murder, Derek Corbally often thought that maybe Jock had just gone into hiding and would breeze back in some day, talking about his next get-rich scheme.

Most importantly, the family had to shield Maureen from the media coverage of her son's death. His face became an icon for gangland brutality. Any time someone died in a shooting or drug-related killing, Jock would be remembered, a paragraph or two about his disappearance and the rumours surrounding his fate reprinted in the daily newspapers.

As far as the family knew, Maureen Corbally never read the graphic accounts of her son's murder that had become common currency in discussions about Dublin crime. There were some things she did not need to know, they reasoned.

In the first searches for the body the family got there before the gardaí. Information came to them first and they went out with shovels to search. The gardaí brought a JCB into one field in Straffan where they were certain the body was buried. The machine dug more than four feet deeper than the average shallow grave and the search area was widened.

Information came in small nuggets to Derek and his brothers. There might be a suggestion about the location of a tree – that the body was between two trees. They tried to get into Judge's mind, looking at the tactics he used to run his drugs business and his way of dealing with situations. Judge would often bury drugs stashes, not trusting anyone to store them for him and not wanting them on his property for fear of searches. He never buried them in fields. Any farmer who knows his land would notice a disturbance, he reasoned. Instead Judge used ditches running alongside main roads. These are easy to get at and any disturbance is less easy to spot. And although farmers walk their land, they do not usually walk their ditches.

Derek Corbally believes his brother's body may have been put into a ditch. Aside from not leaving the telltale dent in the ground that a shallow grave can leave, a ditch would also provide plenty of growth and cover for any disturbance.

Derek Corbally went a long way to try and get answers. As Judge sat in his car in Finglas one day, Derek opened the passenger door and sat in beside him. The criminal jumped, startled that anyone could get so close to him without being spotted. He prided himself on his counter-surveillance skills. When he recognised Derek he calmed slightly.

With his trademark cool demeanour back in place he answered Derek's questions almost politely. He said he had nothing to do with Jock's disappearance. 'He's probably off sunning himself and he'll show up sometime,' Judge said.

The encounter may have been civil, but Judge warned the Corbally family in his own way not to get too close to the truth of what happened to Jock. Some days Judge would drive slowly past Derek's brother's house dozens of times, just so that the target of his low-level intimidation would see him.

The mystery of Jock's whereabouts remains. Derek Corbally believes PJ Judge put a lot of thought into ensuring that Jock would never be found. Dogs, kids, farmers and animals all comb the land at regular intervals and yet Jock's body hasn't been discovered.

All the possible answers to the mystery of Jock's disappearance have been analysed and pondered. Could he be buried in someone else's grave, his family has asked?

Irish attitudes to graves dictate that the soil over a burial plot should never be disturbed, making it one of the safest places to hide something for anyone willing to break that taboo. The gang behind the murder of Veronica Guerin buried weapons in a Dublin graveyard. The location seemed perfect for their needs. Judge had a habit of using graves to hide money.

A body could be buried in a shallow plot above the regulation six feet that gravediggers put between the dead and the living. If the killer was certain that the grave would never be re-excavated, his secret could be safe for decades.

During long hours of searching in the fields of Straffan, Derek has called his dead brother many names. He has asked him to show him a sign. He has put his innate scepticism to one side and has visited psychics. Some of them have told him things about his brother's death that were not in the public domain.

After watching the gardaí at work, the Corbally brothers approached a blacksmith and had metal probes made, just like the ones the experts were using, to search the ground. These devices bring up soil samples, showing whether there are any signs of disturbance. After dozens of hours spent searching, the Corballys have found only dead animals buried illegally by farmers. That evening in Straffan when he thought he might have found Jock's body, Derek understood why search teams are usually made up of people who never knew the person for whom they are looking.

When Maureen Corbally died the family considered giving up the search. The drive to find him was lessened and Derek wondered if he should just leave Jock where he is. Will they ever find Jock? 'I don't know,' is the only answer that Derek gives.

The urge to search for him will probably always be there. The probability that he is buried less than an hour's drive from where he grew up is an added incentive to keep searching. 'It's not as if he's lost in Vietnam, or lost at sea.'

Six months after Jock's murder, PJ Judge was sitting in his car outside the Royal Oak pub in Finglas, close to his family home in Ballygall Crescent, when a gunman walked up to his Ford Fiesta and shot him twice in the head.

Judge was forty-one years old when he died, and suspected of being one of Dublin's biggest heroin dealers. Along with Jock's death, he was a suspect in two other gangland murders.

He was the first one of the men believed to have been involved in Jock Corbally's murder to die.

Nine days later Mark Dwyer, a twenty-three-year-old drug courier, was tortured and murdered by drug dealer 'Cotton Eye' Joe Delaney.

When Delaney was convicted of the murder three years later, trial judge Justice John Quirke described Dwyer's killing as an act of 'unspeakable savagery'. Delaney stood impassively in court as he was sentenced to life for the murder, one of the few convictions in a decade of gangland killings. His conviction was gained on the strength of his son's evidence. Scott Delaney testified against his father and was convicted of a lesser charge in relation to Mark Dwyer's murder.

A former chocolate factory manager, 'Cotton Eye' Delaney had worked as a brothel-keeper and taxi driver before getting into the drugs trade.

In April 2003, a third member of the gang was murdered. Declan Griffin was outside the Horse and Jockey pub in Inchicore on Sunday, 6 April, when he was shot in the back of the head by a lone gunman. At the time of writing a man has been charged with his murder.

Griffin had been bailed out of Mountjoy by his mother five days before his murder. He had been sentenced to six months for possession of offensive weapons and was released pending an appeal. When he had arrived in the prison a self-styled 'welcoming committee' of prisoners had attacked him. He required stitches after the attack.

The attack was the punishment meted out to a tout. Griffin had been at the centre of one of the most dramatic drug trials in criminal history when, in 1999, he was charged with importing heroin and ecstasy.

During the trial Griffin named a member of the Garda National Drugs Unit as his garda handler, and said the garda knew about the drugs he was bringing in when his flight landed in Dublin in December 1995. The 'controlled delivery' went wrong when Customs officials searched Griffin's luggage.

The garda denied that he was running Griffin as an informant. After the dramatic evidence the jury acquitted Griffin on the drugs charges, effectively accepting that he was acting as a drugs mule and an agent of the State. Almost four years later, whatever Griffin knew about his drug business and connections to the gardaí died with him.

Over the years, as the Corbally brothers have searched for Jock in the flat, fertile land around the Kildare village of Straffan, there are others who have made fortunes from these fields.

Site notices and 'sold' signs are springing up on the fences, as builders replace cattle, horses and sheep as the most common occupants of these fields. One dormer bungalow after another dormer bungalow is being built on the sites adjacent to the Naas road. Everything that made it the ideal spot for PJ Judge to bury his victim – its proximity to a main route and its rural attractions – now make it perfect commuter-belt territory.

The Gardaí and the Army dug a whole corner of one field not long after Jock disappeared, convinced that information they had received was spot on. The JCB driver worked late into the evening, so sure were they that Jock was there. Now there are three new houses built on the field. Grass and weeds have grown over the dig, and the new residents are oblivious to the hunt that went on here some years ago.

A stream that was little more than a trickle over a muddy bed when the Corballys first walked along it is now quite a deep waterway, the water pipes from several houses swelling its volume.

In the early days of the search Derek Corbally believes PJ Judge had people watching the family as they searched for Jock, checking to see that they never got too close to the right location. But Derek knows that after more than eight years in the ground or in a ditch, Jock's body would now contain nothing that could identify his killers. Any forensic evidence would have decomposed and been swallowed by the soil. He is hopeful that somebody with accurate knowledge about where his brother is buried will be bothered by their conscience and, at this stage, realise they have nothing to lose by giving up the location.

At a junction in the road, around a mile from the village, the search has narrowed to two large fields. Over one, the Wicklow hills can be seen in the distance. The scene is rural and remote, with only a distant rumble of traffic noise from the dual carriageway.

Although they were city dwellers all their lives, the Corballys now know the ways of Straffan's cattle and other livestock. The cows tend to gather at gates, disturbing the ground when they stand in a herd, waiting and watching. You could bury a body in that patch of ground by a gate in the middle of the night and a farmer would not look twice at the disturbed soil.

The local farmers have accommodated every search, some even offering the help of farm workers. One farmer drained his slurry pit after worms were found there which indicated the possibility of a body in the slime. The Garda sub-aqua unit used special breathing apparatus to search the pit, which was in an area that seemed to match information the family and gardaí had gathered.

The Corballys have several pieces of the puzzle: Jock was buried in an area very close to a house; there was a dog barking that night as the deed was done; a river and the railway line have been mentioned. Locals have told them about seeing people acting suspiciously around the time of the disappearance.

People ask Derek why the Gardaí cannot just dig up all the fields and find Jock. But he understands the difficulties. When you take the size of a body and gauge it in comparison to a field of several acres the task looks impossible. They could spend weeks digging over a field with a full search team, only to have the body lying quietly and unfound just feet away in a verge across the road.

Derek has nothing but praise for the efforts of the Gardaí. Assistant Commissioner Tony Hickey and Detective Inspector Brian Sherry have both impressed him with their efforts to help find Jock's body, the fact that they seemed to take it personally. There have been times when he has phoned Brian Sherry late in the evening and the Inspector has got into his car to go and meet him in some field. As far as Derek is concerned, the senior garda is a credit to the unseen work of a force facing increasing public criticism.

The search has helped to give a focus to their grief, but the difficulty for the family of simply not knowing for sure what happened to Jock is immense. 'Because you don't know the facts of how a person died, your imagination takes over. And in your imagination it's always the most cruel scenario, the most gruesome torture, the most gruesome death. You do imagine the worst, and there's only so much your mind can handle.'

All the possible ways that Judge could have disposed of Jock's body have also been pondered. An animal feed factory in the area was one gruesome thought. Another was a possible link with one of Judge's associates, a Finglas man with a big interest in horses. He could have bought or rented a field and kept horses there without raising too many eyebrows. No-one would take any notice of a horsebox arriving in the field, and there was a lot that could be hidden in a horsebox. Unfortunately, like many of the people Judge surrounded himself with, the man has since been killed.

'He's very close, extremely close,' Derek says of his brother Jock, as he drives the back roads in his car. And how does he feel about the countryside around him on these excursions? 'Ironically, it's very tranquil. If I was going to be buried I wouldn't mind being buried up in Straffan.'

It is just a matter of time, Derek believes, before they find Jock. The development of the fields into sites for housing is one that Judge may not have foreseen in 1996. Some day, as a builder is excavating for the foundations of another house, or a drainage scheme is going into a ditch, they may stumble across something.

'At the end of the day all the family want is to find Jock, put him beside our mother and let him rest.'

Chapter 10

Unravelling the truth

Some small knitted children's jumpers and a man's cardigan are all carefully kept by the Murphy brothers and sisters. They were wrapped in Christmas paper and labelled with the family's names nearly a quarter of a century ago. The giver of these gifts never got to see her dad or her nieces and nephews wearing them.

By the time the family found her presents Phyllis Murphy was dead. The twenty-three-year-old had been out shopping for more Christmas presents the day she disappeared, but the children's jumpers and the cardigan were already bought, wrapped and labelled at home in the Murphy house at Rowanville in Kildare town.

The Murphy family lived with the sinister mystery of Phyllis's murder for two decades – the suspicion that it was someone they knew, someone living in their small town, who had murdered their sister. Over that twenty years, Kildare town has mushroomed into a sprawl of commuter homes and housing estates.

The Murphys feel that Phyllis was working in the background all that time. Just as the presents she bought were unwrapped after she died, the identity of her murderer was revealed long after he killed her. Even the detectives who investigated the case felt there was something beyond the normal run of things influencing events.

It would be going too far to suggest that Phyllis reached out from the grave to point the finger at John Crerar, the former Army sergeant whose children she once minded. But for her family, the timing of the dramatic breakthrough of Crerar's arrest in 1999 – based on DNA evidence which could not have been used twenty years earlier – makes them firmly believe Phyllis had some role in solving the mystery of her death. There were too many minor miracles, too many strokes of luck along the way, for her not to have had a hand in it.

Her family is determined never to let Phyllis be forgotten. During the time between her murder and the breakthrough, a man who was familiar to them had continued to live and work in the same small town. They believe he must have spent nearly twenty years constantly looking over his shoulder. And yet his children grew up as friends of his victim's nieces and nephews.

On Halloween night, 31 October 2002, nearly twenty-three years after Phyllis's death, John Crerar was found guilty of the murder of Phyllis Murphy and sentenced to life in prison. The following afternoon, the day before All Souls' Day, Phyllis's brothers and sisters and four gardaí stood at her graveside to say a decade of the rosary led by the parish priest. They gathered to thank Phyllis for what they saw as her role in putting the mystery of her death finally to rest.

Phyllis was born in September 1956, the third youngest in the family of ten and the quietest baby of the brood. She was christened Philomena, but everyone called her Phyllis from very early on. She would listen quietly to music for hours at a time as the rest of the children came and went in the busy house.

Their father, Michael, had worked with the Army during the Emergency and was now a civilian worker on the Curragh. Their mother, Kathleen, was not a healthy woman. After Phyllis's birth she was hospitalised for three months. Her eldest daughter, Barbara, was only ten years old, but she took time off school to look after the rest of the children.

Barbara believes her mother was training her for what was to come. Before Barbara was seventeen her mother had died, at the age of just forty-one. There was no-one else to do it, so Barbara duly stepped into her mother's shoes, becoming a mother to her younger brothers and sisters. There were nine other children, the youngest just two-and-a-half years old when Kathleen Murphy died.

Phyllis grew up quickly and left school at fifteen to work in various knitwear factories around the area. By the time she was twenty-three she was working as a cutter in Curragh Knitwear, in the nearby town of Newbridge. She loved children and always wanted to work with them.

She lived in digs for part of the working week, with old family friends from the Rowanville estate who had moved to Newbridge. At weekends she would go home to the family house in Kildare.

Phyllis spent the day of 22 December 1979 shopping in Newbridge and pampering herself. She had her hair permed for the first time. She left the hairdresser's delighted with the new hairdo. She was carrying a weekend case with her clothes and toiletries for her stay at home for Christmas, along with a few Christmas presents.

She had not originally intended to get the 6.30 bus that evening. She had been planning to get a later bus and then she and her friend Barbara Luker were to go out for the night to the

CYMS hall in Kildare. But then she found herself laden down with presents and shopping and decided to go home first, catching the earlier bus, to drop off her parcels.

At around four o'clock, just as it was getting dark that evening, she went to visit friends in Newbridge. Then she dropped down to her brother Gerard's house a few doors down. She was in great form, showing off her new hairstyle and looking forward to a great night out.

At the Luker house she told Barbara's mother she would meet Barbara in the CYMS hall as she had to go home with all her stuff first. Mrs Luker walked her up the path of the house to the gate in the dark and waved her off. The bus stop was just a few steps away, opposite the Keadeen Hotel in Newbridge.

Tucked into her dark brown, furry mittens, Phyllis had the 60p bus fare. When the mittens were later found thrown in Colgan's Cut, an area of furze-covered land a few miles down the road, the coins were still nestled at the end of the mitten.

Brendan McArdle and John McManus, two gardaí stationed in Naas, had reason to remember that cold December day. McArdle had a bet on a horse in the 3.30 race. His £2 each-way bet, on a horse called Cobies, came home in style at fifty to one, a once-in-a-lifetime stroke of luck.

A month on from that win, John McManus was the garda who found Phyllis Murphy's body. Nearly twenty years after that, Brendan McArdle would be the garda who found her killer.

At the CYMS hall later that evening, there was no sign of Phyllis. Barbara Luker waited for a while and then went down to Rowanville to find her friend. Straight away the family knew that something was wrong.

On Christmas Eve, RTÉ radio news broadcast a missing persons appeal after gardaí issued a detailed description of Phyllis and where she was last seen. Christmas Day saw the Murphy brothers and friends out searching. Colgan's Cut, beside the chilling plant outside Kildare town, was one of the first areas they searched.

The patch of ground, which has now been cleared for motorway works, was the obvious stopping-off point between Newbridge and Kildare if anyone had taken her from the side of the road. It provided cover for someone who did not want to be seen. Her boots and cardigan were found there the day after she disappeared.

Later the mittens with the 60p would turn up there. Barbara Murphy is convinced that Crerar went back to plant them there, as they were not on the ground when her husband first searched the area. As the search turned towards Wicklow, the Murphy family believe Crerar went back to Colgan's Cut and planted the mittens to draw the searchers away from where he had hidden her body.

There was a randomness to the finds. A week after Christmas, Phyllis's weekend case and some of the presents she had bought were found near Kilcullen. For the first few days her family held out hope that she had been abducted, that she was being held and that someone would release her. It was a slim hope; in their hearts they knew she was probably dead.

On 18 January 1980 Barbara was at home in her newly built house in Melitta Park when news was broadcast on the radio that a woman's body had been found in woods close to the Wicklow Gap. It was the news they had all both hoped for and dreaded. A body meant the wiping out of any last hope that Phyllis had survived. But it also meant a homecoming, a proper burial and some kind of start to finding out what was behind her vanishing. Barbara went straight to Rowanville, where the rest of the family was, and the gardaí had arrived to give them the news.

Her brother Michael identified Phyllis in Naas General Hospital. The Murphy brothers advised their sisters not to see the body. Gerard, the brother she had visited before she disappeared, tried to reassure his sisters that Phyllis had been found clothed. That evening on the six o'clock news, the report stated that her 'naked body' had been found. Gerard and Michael had hoped that kind of detail would not emerge, that they could spare the rest of the family the knowledge of the type of assault she had endured. Looking back now they see how naive they were about it all.

It would emerge later that not just her clothes, but also all her jewellery had been removed before her body was hidden. From the moment the body was found, the gardaí investigating the case thought the murderer must have been someone familiar with forensics, who knew that clothes or jewellery could carry traces of human contact. By stripping her of everything, her killer believed he had left no clues for forensic investigators.

The body did contain one vital clue – a sample of semen left when her attacker raped her. During the post mortem, Professor John Harbison took nine swabs from the body as evidence of a sexual assault. The technology that could unlock the secrets of the bodily fluid had not yet been developed. All that the semen sample could point to in 1979 was a blood type. That information could narrow the list of suspects down to a number of men, but could not positively identify any one person.

In the absence of a witness, a confession or any other supporting evidence, the trace evidence Phyllis's murderer left on her body was a very slim clue. It was a quirk of nature that the material was preserved at all. On the exposed heights of the Wicklow Gap in the depths of winter, the temperature meant the body was effectively frozen in a vast fridge. At another altitude or during another time of the year it would have been lost as the body decomposed.

The search team had gone out to finish the area marked as the boundary of the Carlow/Kildare division. A small stretch of the roadway had to be finished to certify that the area had been searched. That night the hard, cold weather broke. In the darkness that followed all the activity at Ballinagee Bridge as Phyllis was taken from the woods, snow started to fall and the spruce forest was blanketed in white. Had John McManus and the search team not returned that day the snowfall later in the night would have obscured her for days or weeks, during which time decomposition would have slowly destroyed the only clue.

Phyllis's family couldn't help but think that the snow had waited to fall that year.

Phyllis would never have taken a lift from a stranger. This much her family knew. And if she had been forced into the car it would have been difficult to get her and all her baggage in without signs of a struggle, the parcels or her weekend case dropped and left by the side of the road. Barbara thinks now that it was only because she was in such good form and so keen to get home quickly that Phyllis got into Crerar's car. She knew him, but not well and she was cautious.

Phyllis's sister Claire and her husband were friends of the Crerars, and sometimes socialised with them and a third couple.

When Claire and her husband Noel would arrive to go out with John Crerar and his wife Carmel she would usually bring a younger brother or sister to mind the Crerar's children. Sometimes it was Patrick who babysat. Once or twice it was Phyllis.

At the early stage of the investigation the gardaí had no body and no crime scene, other than the Colgan's Cut finds and a few of Phyllis's possessions. There was a strong suspicion that she had been killed by someone she knew. A questionnaire was drawn up and circulated in the town.

On 16 January 1980, two days before her body was found, John Crerar gave a statement to gardaí in Naas Garda Station saying that he did not know the missing woman. When the gardaí checked with the Murphy family they said this was not the case.

'I do not know Phyllis Murphy to speak to. I know her father and sisters Claire and Patricia,' Crerar had said. 'I cannot even remember speaking to Phyllis Murphy in my life.'

There was something odd about his statement and how it conflicted with the Murphy statement. By now he was a serious suspect.

In March that year, as part of a trawl of over fifty men in the area, John Crerar was asked to give a blood sample. At Kildare Garda Station Crerar gave the sample to a local doctor. His blood was smeared on a stain card, a small piece of cardboard slightly larger than a business calling card, with his name and the date written onto it. Forty-nine other men did likewise.

There was a long series of routine interviews to ascertain where the men who were being checked had been on the night Phyllis disappeared. As part of their investigation gardaí interviewed Crerar's fellow security guard at the Black and

Decker factory in Kildare town. Paddy Bolger told them that Crerar had reported for work as night watchman at eight o'clock that evening as normal, and had worked his shift without leaving the factory.

John Crerar kept his secret, and his alibi appeared to be watertight. After two years of activity on the investigation the case slowly stalled. The gardaí had been almost a constant presence in the Murphy house for the first few weeks and months, but then the calls became less frequent as the file went cold.

The Murphy siblings had to get on with their lives, but it was with a certain wariness. If someone they knew had killed Phyllis then he was living alongside them. It was hard to trust anyone and yet it was hard to believe that someone who had done anything like that could be carrying on any kind of normal life.

At night Barbara would lie awake thinking about it over and over again. She would try to remember every detail of who Phyllis knew, racking her memory to see if there was something that she had missed. She couldn't imagine that anyone she knew could have killed her sister. At other times it felt like everyone was a suspect.

For eight years the stain cards with the dried blood of fifty men lay in a wooden cupboard in Naas Garda Station. They had been dried at room temperature, placed with the nine vaginal swabs into a brown envelope and sealed. The cotton swabs were kept in plastic vials about the size of biro casings. The sealed envelope was the responsibility of the exhibits officer assigned to the case. When he retired they were passed to another garda. When the old station was taken out of commission and a new station built the envelope was transferred to another wooden press, along with the dusty ledgers that recorded payments, cheques and routine receipts. The years went on and another exhibits officer retired. At that stage the crucial evidence became the responsibility of the district clerk at Kildare Garda Station, Finbar McPaul.

The samples would spend another nine years in the replacement wooden cupboard, unopened and undisturbed.

Three years after Phyllis was murdered, a fifteen-year-old English schoolgirl called Lynda Mann was raped and murdered in Narborough, a small town in Leicestershire, England. Three years later, in 1986, a second girl, Dawn Ashworth, was also raped and murdered in the area. Semen samples were recovered from both bodies.

The double murder made legal history as the first case in the world where DNA profiles both eliminated the prime suspect and pointed to the murderer. In 1985 three British researchers had demonstrated that DNA could be obtained from crime stains. A comparison of the blood sample from the prime suspect in the Narborough schoolgirl murders and the semen proved that it could not have been him.

So the detectives investigating the schoolgirls' deaths invited all the men in three villages – a total of 5,000 men – to give a blood sample. The ten percent of men with the same blood group as the killer were compared to the semen samples. Still nothing emerged. Then, in a dramatic twist, a woman reported to police how a colleague had boasted at a dinner party that he had masqueraded as his friend to take the test. The friend who had failed to turn up to be tested was local baker Colin Pitchfork. He was arrested and tested and his DNA profile matched the semen from both murders. In 1988 Pitchfork became the first murderer to be convicted on DNA evidence.

DNA or deoxyribonucleic acid is literally the stuff of life. The material found in the nucleus of human cells provides a microscopic genetic code as individual to its owner as a fingerprint. After the Pitchfork case, DNA became a vital tool in forensic crime investigation.

Techniques improved further and in the early 1990s a new way of testing DNA called PCR, or polymerase chain reaction, meant that scientists could obtain a DNA profile result using just tiny traces of bodily matter.

Brendan McArdle joined the Ballistics Section of the Garda Síochána in March 1980. Although ballistics and firearms form part of their work, this section also deals with the wider area of crime scenes and trace evidence. During his years with the section McArdle had worked on three of the most notorious and frustrating missing murder cases, those of schoolboy Philip Cairns, American student Annie McCarrick and the young Kilkenny woman Jo Jo Dullard. A common factor in all three unsolved murders was the lack of a body.

By 1997 McArdle was aware of developments in PCR testing of DNA evidence and started to wonder if the advances could be of any use in other unsolved cases where there might have been something more to go on, in the form of evidence from a body.

He had reason to remember Phyllis Murphy. In January 1980 he had been part of a search team on the Wicklow/Kildare border, on the day before Phyllis's body was found. They called off the search when the light faded. The next day McArdle took the call in Naas Garda Station from the team who found her.

In April 1997 he took the first step that would lead to Phyllis's killer. He picked up the phone and rang Finbar

McPaul in Kildare Garda Station to enquire about the evidence in the Murphy case. In July he drove down to the station and opened the sealed envelope. 'Let's do this formally,' he said. The two men sat down and wrote out a statement recording the handing over of the samples. They each signed it.

Back at Garda Headquarters, the detective handed the swabs over to leading forensic scientist Dr Maureen Smyth for her to ascertain whether anything had survived the seventeen-year interval.

At the Forensic Science Laboratory in Dublin, Dr Smyth ran a fresh analysis on the nine swabs. She advised the detective sergeant that there was enough material to run a DNA profile. The forensic lab did not have the equipment to carry it out, so the swabs would have to be taken to Britain for the first examination.

In March 1998 Brendan McArdle took a flight to Heathrow with the samples in his briefcase. He hired a car and drove to Oxfordshire.

In the town of Abingdon a successful biotechnology firm was cornering the market in a growing business. Cellmark Diagnostics had been set up in 1987. It was primarily a commercial DNA testing facility, where the main business was paternity testing.

The detective handed the nine swabs over to Cellmark forensic scientist Matthew Greenhalgh. In April 1998 word came back that a full DNA profile had been obtained.

Garda administration then became a factor as Detective Sergeant McArdle applied for the funds to have the blood samples from the suspects tested. In September 1998 he took twenty-three of the stain cards from the Murphy case envelope to Abingdon to have them compared to the semen DNA profile.

There was no breakthrough. A second lot of the old stain cards were taken to Abingdon, along with twelve new samples from men who had been recalled.

The second batch of tests proved conclusively that a man whom gardaí had considered for years as the prime suspect for the murder was in fact innocent. His sample was among the batch of new blood tests. It seemed there was to be no breakthrough. The budget for testing was spent and support for Brendan McArdle's quest was dwindling.

There were ten old stain cards left.

In June 1999 the detective sergeant was on the beach in Templetown, County Louth, organising the search for another missing woman murder victim. The IRA had said that Belfast mother-of-ten Jean McConville had been buried in the area. This search for Jean McConville would prove fruitless. It was August 2003, four years later, when her body was found by a man walking with children, at a sandbank on nearby Shelling Hill beach, not Templetown as the IRA had indicated.

At 3.15 that afternoon in 1999, McArdle took a call on his mobile phone. The last ten cards had been analysed and there had been a match. The name on the card was John Crerar. The detective made three phone calls to his Garda bosses. The last call was to Assistant Commissioner Tony Hickey. 'Do you think this man is still alive?' Hickey asked him.

Not only was John Crerar alive, but every witness that was interviewed originally – who would be required to mount a successful prosecution against him – was also still alive.

The only problem was that Crerar had an alibi. The trial would hear later that Paddy Bolger had lied when he was first questioned. Claiming to have been afraid that he might lose his job, Bolger had said that Crerar had arrived for work when he was supposed to, at 8pm. If that was true Crerar would not have had time to carry out the rape and murder.

Questioned again by gardaí in 1999, Paddy Bolger said that Crerar had turned up briefly for work at 9pm and left immediately. And he told gardaí that Crerar did not return for nearly two hours. This made more sense and left Crerar ample time to dispose of Phyllis's body and her clothing.

The file was sent to the DPP's office with the new DNA evidence.

On Tuesday, 13 July 1999, the gardaí asked the Murphy family to gather together and gave them the news that a suspect had been arrested in connection with Phyllis's murder. That morning, shortly before 7.30am, gardaí had gone to Crerar's workplace, the Sheshoon Stud at Maddenstown, and taken him into custody in Naas Garda Station when he arrived for work. Crerar gave another blood sample voluntarily and it was sent to the Forensic Science Laboratory, where PCR testing equipment was now in place. That evening the DPP gave instructions to charge Crerar with murder.

Barbara and the rest of the Murphys were shocked. They knew he had been questioned about Phyllis at the time of the murder, but his alibi had made them believe that he was innocent.

Barbara knew Crerar to say 'hello' to. She considered him a loner. He was a figure always in the background, inconspicuous in the town, known by most people as a quiet and strange man. Rumours about an unhealthy interest in women and unresolved allegations of a sexual assault had put him under something of a cloud. But had it not been for the DNA match, his horrible secret would probably never have been revealed.

Two of the Murphy family were in Australia, and another brother was on his way to work in Dublin when the news broke on the radio. He heard it from work colleagues.

The following day Crerar made a brief appearance at Naas District Court. As he was led handcuffed from an unmarked Garda car a large crowd of angry people shouted 'murderer' at him and jostled him. By the time he emerged from the court the crowd had almost doubled. The public was fascinated to see what the murder suspect looked like after all these years.

Barbara Murphy and her family did not go to court that day. They knew what Crerar looked like and they knew there would be a circus outside the court. They waited until the fuss had died down to attend the court hearings.

Later that month at the High Court, Crerar got bail. As a condition of his release from prison he was told to reside in Dublin and sign on at a local Garda station. He was banned from applying for a passport and told not to make any contact with any witnesses.

After the initial commotion around the case, things went quiet again. It seemed that every time it looked like there would be a date set for the trial things went wrong. In April 2002, nearly two years after Crerar was first charged, the trial was adjourned again.

Sitting in the Central Criminal Court, Judge Paul Carney remarked that he had received a lot of representations about the case. He commented also that he was worried about delays in murder cases caused by a shortage of judges.

Crerar's trial was originally listed to start in February 2002. Gerard Murphy was several thousand feet in the air on a flight home from Australia when the court heard that there would have to be a further adjournment. He had organised to be home for a month, but had to return to Australia without seeing the trial start.

The Murphy family wrote to Judge Carney and to the president of the High Court about the ongoing delays, and the judge said he would list it for the first day of the following legal term.

But on the day it was due to start the court heard that one of the main garda witnesses had suffered a heart attack. The trial had to be further adjourned, to the end of the list, in order to allow the witness to attend the trial.

Eventually on Tuesday, 8 October 2002, prosecution counsel Michael Durack SC got to his feet in the Central Criminal Court and outlined the State's case against John Crerar. There were two planks to the prosecution – the withdrawal of Crerar's alibi for his whereabouts on the night Phyllis disappeared, and the link that had been made between Crerar and his victim by both Cellmark Diagnostics and the new sample Crerar had given which was tested by the Forensic Science Laboratory.

Barbara Murphy travelled to court every day, along with her brothers and sisters. She looked at the predominantly young jury and hoped that they would follow the complex scientific evidence they were about to hear.

Her fears that the evidence would be too technical for a lay audience were allayed by the testimony of Dr Maureen Smyth. The forensic scientist outlined in precise and clearly comprehensible terms the reliability of DNA evidence in identifying a rapist.

Alongside the young jury, there were quite a few grey heads and receding hairlines in the courtroom. The Murphys dubbed them Dad's Army, all the retired detectives who turned up to finally see the trial in a murder case that had doggedly refused to go away.

The gardaí kept the family well informed of what was happening in the case, providing huge support during the three weeks of the trial. Brendan McArdle, the detective sergeant who had reopened the case, was now a detective inspector with the Ballistics Section.

There was another man in court who had made contact with the Murphys earlier that year. Sometime around January, Barbara heard that there was a man making inquiries about her late mother through social workers in the town. With all the drama of the trial, it seemed strange that something like that would be going on in the background.

The man was Paul Delaney. He had grown up in Carlow with an adoptive family. When he reached his fifties he decided to try and trace his mother. It emerged that he was Kathleen Murphy's first son. Born three years before Barbara, a local priest had arranged that he be given to a family in Carlow so that Kathleen would not have to bring him up on her own. There was no formal adoption, but when he got married Paul took on the name Delaney, the family name of the couple who had reared him.

The authorities had decided not to break the news to the Murphy family until after the trial was over. But there were ongoing adjournments and when Barbara looked into all the queries about her mother, the Murphys discovered that they had a brother they never knew.

The revelation of a long-lost brother as they faced into the trial for the murder of their sister helped the family to get over the disappointment of yet another adjournment.

The only one who had known Kathleen Murphy's secret was her own sister, who was still alive and living in England. She knew that Kathleen had had a son, had called him Paul, and had given him up.

The family of ten who had lost one became a family of ten again. Paul Delaney went to the trial on a number of days to hear about the last days in the life of the younger sister that he never met.

Halloween was the second day the jury had spent deliberating, and the wait was exhausting. Late that evening they returned with a verdict. Until the word 'guilty' was spoken the Murphys did not know how it would go. It was almost twenty-three years since Phyllis had disappeared, and finally they had some answers.

In the Ormond Hotel beside the Four Courts they had a drink and some tea and coffee with the gardaí and then it was home to Kildare later that night.

The next day Barbara felt the stress of the three-week trial and the aftershock of years of anxiety crowd in on her. At the graveside the family said a decade of the rosary for Phyllis. Later that evening Barbara went on the 'Late Late Show' to talk about the case. They had always wanted to speak about Phyllis to the media. It was a way of keeping her name alive and reminding people of the case. For the Murphys, it also ensured that her real story was aired, and not some distorted version of it.

They think about her every day. She was watching things, Barbara believes. And she was a constant presence.

Barbara often thinks about the families of the women who disappeared in the Leinster area in the years after Phyllis's murder. She lived through a month of not knowing what had happened to her sister, hoping desperately she was alive and then, as time went on, hoping that they would find her body. But even she cannot begin to imagine what those families feel.

If Phyllis's body had not been found she thinks the family would still be looking even nearly a quarter of a century later. Her jewellery was never found. Perhaps Crerar buried it somewhere. The remains of a fire were found with some of the clothes she had been wearing.

Phyllis Murphy would have been forty-eight in September 2004. The likelihood is she would have been wrapping Christmas presents for her own children over the years, and maybe even by now grandchildren.

The Murphys did not get any bereavement counselling. A close-knit family, they leaned on each other for support. 'Every day I think about her,' says Barbara. 'We talk about her all the time. We don't ever not talk. Some people worry about bringing up her name. But we bring it up and put them at their ease, because why not talk about her? She had a short life so we have to keep it going for her.'

Chapter 11

Two Latin words
– Nolle prosequi

Aisling McCarthy came barrelling out of the garda station that morning with one thought in her head. For hours she had been sitting on the hard chairs in Coolock station giving statements, line by line. It was painful and slow as one detective and then another wrote the words in longhand on the ruled pages. As she left in the early morning, angry and frustrated, she turned and shouted back at the station door, 'You wait until I tell me ma.'

Aisling told her ma about everything. They went to the pub together, went to the movies like sisters and giggled about everything from work to her mother's love of chocolate and her morning cigarette.

As soon as the words were out, Aisling realised the cold reality of that morning. Joan McCarthy wasn't around to listen to her daughter's woes over tea and a biscuit. She had been found in Aisling's spare room in Edenmore, north Dublin, just days earlier. She was lying dead on the bed with the duvet pulled up around her face. And Aisling, her eldest daughter, had just been released after hours of questioning about her death.

Five years after the night in April 1998 when Joan McCarthy died, a jury at Dublin's Coroner's Court returned a verdict of unlawful killing. It is the only verdict that has been handed down in relation to the forty-six-year-old Dublin woman's death. Her family has been left wondering what happened during the investigation into her death? How did Joan McCarthy die, and why did they feel they were torn apart by the investigation process and led to the steps of the criminal courts, only to have all doors slam closed in their faces?

Joan was Bridget Ward's eldest child and only daughter. Six sons followed her small chatty girl in the family home in Raheny, north Dublin. Joan went to school in St Ita's in Raheny and her parents had enrolled her in the Marino Technical School. But at fourteen she got the taste of holiday work and the money she could make. She started working as a machinist. Much of it was piece-work, where the young girls were paid by item. The harder you worked the more you took home at the end of a shift. Joan became an over-locker, putting the over-locking seams in clothes in factories around Dublin.

She was a jobbing machinist, going where the work was. If word came round on a lunch break that another factory was paying more, the girls would leave the job and go to the next one.

At a dance she met Charlie McCarthy, the man she would marry. Aisling was their eldest child and then, a few years later, the twins Jennifer and Joanne were born. The dynamics of the family meant that Aisling and Joan were always close. The twins had each other. Aisling had her ma.

In a house full of women, they poked gentle fun at Charlie. Bridget Ward still remembers her then-future son-in-law arriving up to take Joan out, looking thin as a match and with a different suit on him every time. There was the time after they got married that he presented Joan with a Valentine card. The only problem with the card was that it was a card that a woman would give to a man. Then there was the time when

Joan sent him out for two Kit Kats; he came back with two cans of Kitekat cat food. They didn't even have a cat.

Now Aisling and her grandmother can see the emptiness in Charlie McCarthy. He cannot talk about his dead wife without weeping. The weight of the loss and loneliness has felled him. Now the women have to mind him.

In February 1998 Bridget Ward decided that an important photograph had to be taken. Bridget's mother was in a nursing home and had not been well. Her great-granddaughter Gemma, Aisling's daughter, was nearly two. She did not know how much longer there would be five generations – four women and a baby – sharing the same time in the world. So the photograph of the dynasty was arranged. There they were: Granny Coughlan, Bridget, Joan, Aisling and her toddler daughter Gemma.

At her place in the middle of the five generations, Joan was in the unusual position of being both a grandmother and a granddaughter. Two months later it was Joan who was dead. The woman that they were worried would not live much longer was not the first face to be lost from the picture of the five generations. Despite the elderly lady's ill health, Joan McCarthy's grandmother outlived her.

Looking back now at those weeks before Joan McCarthy's death, her mother and daughter see significance in the smallest things. At a light-hearted visit to a fortune teller before she died, Joan was told that she had an enemy and that she would be receiving a lot of flowers. With the twins' twenty-first coming up, she put the flowers down to the party they were planning. When she would be getting ready to go out she would joke about having to watch her back because of this mysterious enemy.

It was Holy Week in April 1998 when the last few days of her life were played out. On the night before her death Bridget, Joan and Aisling went to see the blockbuster movie *Titanic*. As they came out of the cinema that night it poured out of the heavens. The three of them laughed at the watery end to the night.

On Good Friday Aisling planned to go to a house in Kilbarrack where a few friends were getting together for a card game because the pubs would be closed. She picked up her mother after work at lunchtime and they went shopping and had a bite of lunch in Raheny. Joan planned to invite a friend around to Aisling's house that night as she babysat Gemma.

At around eleven o'clock that Good Friday night Joan spoke to her mother on the phone. She told Bridget she was about to go to bed and would bring a hot water bottle with her. She must have changed her mind as a film caught her eye on the television. She sat up and watched *Sleeping with the Enemy* and then headed up the stairs in the small, neat house, talking to Charlie on the phone before she went off to sleep.

Later that night Aisling and her fiancé Brian Farrell arrived home. In the early hours of the morning, around 3.00am, Aisling went in to her mother and they chatted briefly. Gemma had just been moved out of her cot to her own bed, and Joan told Aisling that the child had fallen out of the bed, but was fine.

On Easter Saturday Aisling woke to find her heating had switched itself on. The house was like a sauna. The switch had been giving trouble, so she sent Brian out to turn the heat off at the mains, in the shed at the back of the garden. She got out of bed and crossed the landing into the spare room, to get some clothes out of the wardrobes in there. She saw her mother lying with her head between two pillows. That was unusual, as Joan always slept on top of two pillows, one on top of the other. The duvet was pulled up around her neck and ears and just an oval of the side of her face was showing. When Aisling took a closer look, the shock sent her reeling back against the bedroom wall. Her mother's face was blue. Against the sheets it was a blue so dark it was almost black.

At that instant she heard the thud of Gemma's feet, as the toddler ran towards her grandmother's bed to launch herself on Joan. Aisling reached down and grabbed her daughter and brought her out of the room, running with her downstairs to keep her from seeing her grandmother. The ambulance was called just after 10am and the paramedics from Kilbarrack Fire Station came to the scene.

Firefighter Larry McGivern arrived to find the body of a woman lying in the double bed, covered by the duvet. He checked for a pulse and found none, but the body was still warm. Along with his ambulance partner Paddy Galligan, they carried Joan out on a carrying sheet. As they manoeuvred her onto the sheet they noticed that rigor mortis had already started to set in.

Then the family rushed to Beaumont Hospital. When he got the panicked phone call, Charlie McCarthy came running across the field that separated Aisling's house from her mother's. On the dash over he slipped and fell. As he rounded the last corner the ambulance passed him on the way to the hospital.

Joan McCarthy was pronounced dead by Dr Cathy McHugh at the accident and emergency department of Beaumont Hospital that morning, 11 April 1998. Dr McHugh noted that her head was very purple but there was a clean line on her neck. She noted a mark on her neck and a graze on her right shoulder. There was blood in Joan's hair on the left side of her head.

At 11.30am Charlie identified his wife's body. In the relatives' room in Beaumont, the McCarthy family were told by a nurse that the gardaí would be coming to talk to them, as was routine in the case of a sudden death. Aisling was allowed in to see her mother's body. Then the two gardaí, Detective Inspector William Redmond and Detective Sergeant Cathal Cryan, arrived.

Meanwhile, about an hour after the ambulance left, gardaí arrived at Aisling's three-bedroomed terraced house at Millwood Villas in Donaghmede and began to seal off the house. The initial report from the hospital was enough to prompt an investigation into Joan McCarthy's death. The house, the bedroom and everything in it were now part of a potential crime scene.

The family went to Joan and Charlie's house. That evening Inspector Redmond, who was leading the investigation, told them that Joan had not died naturally. Aisling was asked to come to the station.

She sat in the Garda station giving statements until the early hours. Then she went home, but had to go back to the station the next day to finish her statement. A few days later, Aisling and her partner Brian Farrell were both arrested. During her detention Aisling McCarthy says gardaí showed her photographs from Joan McCarthy's post mortem. She saw a picture of her mother's skull peeled back. Another photograph showed a hand holding a human brain.

She can recall every detail of the photographs. Sometimes when she closes her eyes they flash across her mind.

She can understand that the gardaí used certain tactics in questioning suspects in what appeared to be a murder case. That does not make it any easier to forget the stark images of the post mortem.

On Friday, 24 September 1999, seventeen months after Joan McCarthy's death, Aisling's by-now-former partner Brian Farrell was charged with the murder. Aisling and Brian Farrell's relationship had broken up and he was no longer living in Millwood Villas. At the brief appearance at Dublin District Court, the twenty-four-year-old with an address at Foxhill Park, Coolock, was remanded in custody to appear again the following week.

Aisling had been told by gardaí the evening before that there might be news. The next morning she heard about the murder charge against her former partner on the radio headlines in the sewing factory where she was working, surrounded by workmates.

After the shock of her mother's death, she was now preparing to face into the trial of her daughter's father, her former partner.

A provisional trial date was set for October 2000. The Friday before the expected start of the trial Aisling went to Donaghmede to buy clothes and shoes for court. She got a call to go to her mother's house. Here, the family was told by gardaí that the trial was not going ahead on that date, but another date would be set. A date for the following summer was set down.

But just before the trial was due to start, Charlie McCarthy was asked to call up to the Garda station, where he was told that the state would be entering a *nolle prosequi*. The Latin phrase, literally translated as 'do not pursue', records the decision not to proceed with a prosecution. The term can be used as a verb. To *nolle prosequi* is to declare that a legal case will not be prosecuted.

The news came out of the blue. It was the last thing they expected. They had no inkling that there were any obstacles to a prosecution, and had no idea that there had been any major difficulties during the investigation.

No explanation was given to the McCarthy family. No-one could tell them how or why the case had been pursued almost to the steps of the Four Courts and then dropped. The decision had been taken by the DPP, the McCarthy family was told. After the wave of emotion and tension in the run-up to a murder trial, now they were left dumbfounded, confused and completely in the dark.

What Joan McCarthy's relatives did not know then was that an extraordinary clash of opinions had happened behind the scenes, between the principal detectives investigating her death. The simmering dispute had led to one detective sergeant making a formal complaint to Garda management that a murder investigation had been launched without sufficient evidence to prove that there had been a murder.

After the case was dropped there was an internal inquiry, the findings of which were never made public, and eventually an inquest, which would raise as many questions as it answered. An extensive Garda inquiry had ended with the DPP effectively stopping the prosecution at the eleventh hour. At the end of the long and arduous process for her family, Joan McCarthy's death would remain a mystery.

As far as the McCarthy family was concerned up to that point, the Garda investigation was progressing as it should. Members of the force were working together to solve the questions surrounding Joan McCarthy's death, to ascertain if anyone was responsible and, if so, to make that individual accountable.

But behind the scenes the investigation team had fractured, with two of the detectives disagreeing bitterly over the medical evidence and its level of support for a murder charge.

Detective Inspector William Redmond and Detective Sergeant Cathal Cryan were the first gardaí to see Joan McCarthy's body, when they were summoned to Beaumont Hospital on Easter Saturday 1998 by a member of the nursing staff.

From the hospital, the two gardaí went to Millwood Villas and did a preliminary examination of the back bedroom where the body had been found. Later that day Inspector Redmond went to the morgue. He was present at the post mortem carried out by the State Pathologist, Professor John Harbison.

The examination found that Joan McCarthy had suffered extensive bruising on her neck and a fracture of the hyoid bone, a small bone in the throat, as well as fracturing of the thyroid cartilage. These were compression injuries, that had resulted in her death from asphyxiation.

As a result of the findings of the post mortem, Inspector Redmond declared the case a murder inquiry. That evening he told Joan McCarthy's shocked family that their mother, sister, daughter and wife had not died naturally. It was, as far as the gardaí were now concerned, a case of murder.

Until that time, Joan McCarthy's passing was in the category of 'suspicious death'. This term is used where it appears that a person, in otherwise good health, has suffered some kind of injury and died. In some cases the death is found to have been an accident, or attributable to some hitherto unknown medical cause. In other cases the death is upgraded from a suspicious death to a homicide investigation.

The machinery of the Garda Síochána that starts to work once such an investigation is launched takes on a momentum of its own. An incident room or area is set up in the Garda station nearest the location of the death. Gardaí are assigned to the investigation from other duties; phone lines can be set up, with members of the force assigned to them; house-to-house inquiries are undertaken; public appeals are made for information; hundreds of statements are written up painstakingly by hand. Many hours are clocked up and much overtime is used. In the end a book of evidence, containing the work of the inquiry team, is forwarded to the Director of Public Prosecutions, who ultimately decides whether to prosecute a suspect or suspects for the murder.

According to his final report the then state pathologist, Professor John Harbison, was taken to the scene at Millwood Villas on the night of Easter Saturday after he had finished the post mortem on the body.

Written in his usual formal and forensic manner, the veteran state pathologist's final report describes the scene that he and the gardaí encountered that evening: 'Inside the house I was conducted up the stairs to the back bedroom, in which my interest lay in any irregular object with which the deceased's face and neck could have been in forcible contact. The only possibilities were a trouser press lying on its side beside the pillow on the window side of the bed and a headboard of a bed, apparently of wrought iron. Beside this was the back of a chair, the top of which was at about the level of my belt. The bedhead was only one inch to two inches higher. On the near side of the bed was a built-in wardrobe with a centre dressing table unit on which was a hair brush, talcum powder and other toiletries. Also on it was a glass with about an inch of water in the bottom.'

The wrought-iron headboard was from another bed, and not the bed in which Joan McCarthy had been sleeping. It was among items of furniture Aisling was storing for Brian Farrell's sister. The furniture had been stacked up on the right-hand side of the double bed where Joan had been found dead.

Harbison's report, dated 19 June 1998, concluded that while the asphyxia that killed Joan McCarthy was due to strangulation, the 'markings on the neck were not typical either of manual strangulation, there being no fingernail marks on the skin of her neck, or of ligature strangulation … [I] therefore formed the opinion that either an irregular-shaped object or series of objects were pressed against the deceased's neck or that she had her neck pressed from behind against some irregular structure or structures.'

In other words, it was not a pair of hands or a rope that was used to strangle Joan McCarthy. Something was pressed against her neck, or she was pressed against something by somebody who gripped her from behind.

The theory that Joan McCarthy might have died accidentally after falling forward and injuring her neck on something was excluded in Professor Harbison's report because of the absence of any alcohol in her blood. 'Mrs McCarthy was not under the influence of any alcoholic drink, which does not readily allow her death to be explained by a fall forwards on her neck, that is postural asphyxia,' Professor Harbison stated.

It was this issue of alcohol – the crucial factor in the conclusion that Joan McCarthy's death had not been an accident – that led to confusion for her family.

Aisling knew her mother had brought over some Bacardi in a bottle, to have a drink with a friend who was due to call that night. When the friend cancelled she believes her mother did not have anything to drink. A half-empty bottle was found on the kitchen counter.

Toxicology tests on her blood and urine found that Joan McCarthy had no drugs or alcohol in her system when she died. It appeared that the Bacardi bottle was half-empty because she had brought it around to the house like that.

The family had been given different accounts of the whereabouts and condition of the bottle. One member of the investigation team told them the bottle had been emptied and washed out, with Diet Coke cans thrown in the bin and a glass washed and wiped after use. They still wonder, if that was not the case, then why were they told so?

When the case ended so abruptly, Bridget Ward and Aisling McCarthy started asking questions. They were met with a blank wall. 'Don't contact my office again,' was the response from the DPP's office. 'That's my final word.' But they wanted someone to sit down at a table with them and explain what had happened. After repeated requests for a copy of the post mortem report on her mother's death, Aisling was given a single sheet recording the cause of death. Later she received a four-page document, and then finally an eight-page report.

The difficulties in getting information and answers had the combined effect of wearing down the family and making them increasingly inquisitive. If there was nothing to hide, why were they being given the runaround, they wondered?

Finally in July 2003, more than five years after the death, an inquest was opened in the Dublin Coroner's Court under Dr

Brian Farrell. The family had persisted in requesting an inquest, pushing for any forum that would give some kind of answers about Joan McCarthy's death.

During the inquest Inspector William Redmond explained his decision to launch a murder inquiry. 'I did not make a premature conclusion,' he stated in his handwritten deposition to the inquest.

'As a result of PM [post mortem] I commenced murder investigation,' Inspector Redmond's deposition reads. 'I didn't tell Dr Harbison that deceased had taken alcohol. I told him alcohol may have been consumed. Never a question of accidental fall. Dr Harbison never mentioned it to me on the 11th April.'

But the rift that had been a feature of the investigation from the start emerged during the inquest into the death. From the beginning of the investigation Detective Sergeant Cryan had kept a detailed record of his recall of the events. By the time the inquest was convened he had retired from the force.

In his statement to the Coroner's Court he recalled Easter Saturday 1998, when the death was first reported. He described viewing the body at Beaumont. 'I did notice a number of what appeared to be superficial wounds or scratches on her neck and shoulders.' He said both he and Inspector Redmond agreed it was a suspicious death that should be reported to the coroner.

Back at the bedroom where she had been found, Sergeant Cryan noted the same scene recorded in the Harbison report, with furniture stacked up against one side of the bed where Joan McCarthy was found. 'These items included a wrought-iron headboard and an electric freestanding trouser press and a large vase. The trouser press and wrought-iron headboard appeared to have been originally stacked up-right, right up against the side of the bed, but were now lying on their side.'

Although he agreed with the initial decision to declare the death suspicious, Sergeant Cryan did not agree that only one conclusion could be arrived at after the post mortem. From the earliest stage of the investigation he had what he described in a report as 'grave doubts' about the level of support in the post mortem for a murder charge.

Unbeknownst to the family, towards the end of 1998 Sergeant Cryan sought a meeting with the investigation team to clarify the issues he believed were raised by the Harbison report, and the fact that he believed the post mortem findings did not rule out the possibility of an accidental fall.

On Tuesday, 8 December 1998, in Santry station, Sergeant Cryan told a conference of the investigation team of his reservations about the evidence. The most senior officer at the conference told the sergeant to seek a meeting with Dr Harbison. The next day the sergeant and a detective superintendent sat for over two hours in Dr Harbison's office in Trinity College.

According to a report Sergeant Cryan wrote up about the affair, which he subsequently forwarded to the Chief State Solicitor's Office, the sergeant told the pathologist at this meeting that he was concerned about a potential miscarriage of justice. He said that Dr Harbison agreed that his findings could point to how Joan McCarthy died – from asphyxiation by compression of her neck – but the pathologist did not know what object was responsible or how this object came into contact with her neck.

According to Sergeant Cryan's interpretation of Harbison's post mortem report, it left open the possibility that

Joan McCarthy had sustained her injuries in a fall. In medical terms this could be described as postural asphyxia. It was only the absence of alcohol in her system, the detective argued, that led Professor Harbison to rule out the possibility of postural asphyxia.

The one imponderable was how she could have been found in the bed with the duvet pulled up over her if she had indeed died after a fall.

Sergeant Cryan recorded the events in a report which he sent to the DPP in January 2000. Aisling's former partner Brian Farrell had been charged with murder and was awaiting trial when the report arrived at the law officers' desks.

None of the McCarthy family knows what, if anything, the Cryan report had to do with the decision of the DPP to withdraw the prosecution against Brian Farrell. It is not known, outside of the small circle of people involved in the case in the DPP's office, whether the report was even received or read by the DPP.

The family was represented at the inquest by solicitor Michael Finucane. When he questioned the toxicology tests during cross-examination of Professor Harbison, the pathologist reacted angrily. He said that it was a 'ferocious allegation' to make to question the accuracy of the alcohol tests. And besides, Professor Harbison said, there would have been a smell of alcohol at the post mortem.

In his evidence to the court, Professor Harbison said: 'I came to the conclusion that she died from asphyxia due to strangulation due to compression at the front of the neck by pressure from object or objects unknown or pressure by the neck against an object or objects unknown to the best of my knowledge.'

The coroner, Dr Brian Farrell, asked if Professor Harbison's findings implied a third-party strangulation.

'I regret they do, coroner,' the pathologist answered.

The repercussions from the dispute between investigators went up to the top of the system. An internal Garda inquiry was ordered into Sergeant Cryan's concerns about how the McCarthy death was investigated. Chief Superintendent John Long was appointed to carry out the internal investigation. Its results were never made public.

In a letter to Michael Finucane in February 2004 Deputy Commissioner Fachtna Murphy gave a one-line synopsis of the findings of that inquiry: 'Chief Superintendent Long has concluded that the Garda investigation was thorough in every respect.'

In response to her letter to the DPP Bridget Ward received a reply which shed little light on what went on at the meeting at which it was decided to enter a *nolle prosequi*. 'The file was personally considered by the Director [of Public Prosecutions], in consultation with two senior counsel engaged on behalf of the prosecution, prior to the decision being made to discontinue the proceedings ... I can assure you that the decision to discontinue the prosecution was arrived at very reluctantly and only after a careful evaluation of all of the evidence,' the letter from Deputy Director Barry Donoghue stated.

No explanation was forthcoming about the background to the DPP's initial decision to charge Brian Farrell in the first place.

The DPP has since stated that there has been no new evidence and, despite the recording of a verdict of 'unlawful killing' by the inquest, it would not be possible for him to change his decision in relation to a prosecution.

Aisling McCarthy knows that she and her gran have a reputation in the family as two strong women. They are the ones who are expected to hold things together. When she talks about her mother she automatically smiles at the memory of the life they shared. Alone at home at night she is less able to grit her teeth and carry off the tough exterior.

Bridget Ward still feels the loss of her daughter like a physical jolt. She describes it as a sob that springs from her heart into her throat with no warning every day. It causes her to catch her breath.

Her boys are good sons, but her daughter would have looked after her as she believes only a daughter can. They had their squabbles, Bridget and Joan. Bridget's hot-headedness has passed down through Joan to Aisling. Bridget and Aisling are angry that they have been told so little about the State's handling of the death of Joan McCarthy in April 1998. The response of the authorities is that, in the absence of any new evidence, the investigation will not be reopened.

Family solicitor Michael Finucane believes the family, the three generations of an ordinary extended Dublin family living within walking distance of each other's homes all their lives, may be entitled to a proper investigation under the European Convention on Human Rights.

Until then the family says the system has failed them.

Chapter 12
Seven years for two lives

The two men had never met until their lives violently collided in north London one February night. One of them, Noel Neville, was like thousands of other young Irish men in the city. He worked as a bricklayer, a member of the green army of brickies, plasterers, labourers and shovel men that built so much of the prosperous European capital.

The details about the other man are sketchier. On paper he was Mr Normal, albeit with a slightly unusual surname. Leslie Tobutt was forty-two, with a comfortable life, working as an electronics engineer for British Airways. Under the surface, though, things were not good. His marriage was over. Although they lived under the same roof, he led a separate life from his wife Kate and their three children and she was filing for divorce.

Noel was twenty-nine, doing another stint of building work in London, living in Harrow and enjoying life. He was not a man to make any huge plans for the future. London was always going to be temporary and now he had definite thoughts of returning home.

It was 1992. On his Christmas visit home to Skryne in County Meath, there had been a smell of better times in the air. The building industry was starting to rumble into life again after the recession years of the 1980s. No-one knew it then, but a boom was on the way that would end with the Irish building industry importing instead of exporting its labour.

But Noel Neville never made it home to enjoy the boom years. On the night of 4 February 1992, Noel was in the Tobutt home in North London when Leslie Tobutt burst in. Tobutt stabbed Noel to death, along with his own wife Kate, in an appallingly violent and frenzied attack.

Noel Neville, the eldest of five boys, was killed by a man whose face he may only have vaguely noticed in his new girlfriend's family pictures. His family were left to deal with the trauma of their son and brother dying in a so-called crime of passion. The awful event shattered the lives of his brothers and his mother. The Neville family have never recovered.

Liam Neville had just arrived in London for a brief holiday visit on the night his brother died. He had travelled to Ealing to stay with another brother, Tommy. That night they got the call from the uncle with whom Noel was staying to say that Noel had been stabbed, that Noel was dead.

In the numbness and shock of disbelief there was the huge problem of how to break the news to their mother. Margaret Neville had already had two dreadful events in her life. In 1985 one of her sons was in a terrible car accident. He had been put on a life-support machine and had to undergo medical treatment for a further two years, which was to change the course of his life. After that she was left coping with the effects of a serious brain injury.

In 1986 her husband, who was not yet fifty, dropped dead following a heart attack. A young widow, Margaret Neville had already almost lost a son and said goodbye forever to the father of her five boys.

Liam and Tommy rang a neighbour in the Meath village. The local priest was called upon to visit the Neville house and deliver the terrible news.

When Margaret Neville arrived in London, the family had been told they could view the body. Noel was laid out with a sheet covering his body, with just his head uncovered. He had suffered multiple stab wounds. To Liam's abiding horror, British police offered to show them the knife. He was given a bag with what was left of the clothes that Noel was wearing that night.

He accompanied Margaret in to say goodbye to her son. They were asked not to touch Noel's body. She was not able to hold his hand and say goodbye. There was no way for his mother to put meaning on her son's death. Nothing about his death made any sense. Losing her child was something she had never expected to endure.

To lose Noel in the way they did brought with it an added burden. Media interest in the murder was instant and over-whelming. When Liam heard that reporters had called to the family home in Meath he was incensed. As far as he was concerned the press refused to take 'no' for an answer. The intrusion was difficult to take.

Worse was to come. British tabloids seized on the details of how Tobutt came to commit the double killing.

The police told Liam that Noel and Kate had been sitting together having a cup of coffee in her front room, with her children present, when Leslie Tobutt burst in. The trial would hear allegations that Tobutt saw the couple engaged in a sexual act. Noel and Kate Tobutt were not alive to tell their side of the story. The sex angle suited the defence position that Leslie Tobutt had been blinded by rage at what he saw.

The tabloids went to town with all the lurid details from the trial. The reporting hurt the family all over again.

Through the numbness and shock that descended on them as a family, Liam focused his anger on the media. Alongside the press interest he found there was a fascination among people at large for the gory details of his brother's death.

It was a stigma, he felt, to have lost a brother to murder. The fact that Noel was killed by a jealous husband exacerbated the stigma. It was a horrendous thought that people all over Ireland and Britain were talking about the killing over pints and cups of coffee. At the same time Liam felt that people were avoiding him, almost embarrassed to speak to him. The label of a murder victim's brother was a difficult one to carry around in a small Irish village.

Liam had not spoken to his brother about the relationship with Kate, who worked as a nurse. Like most young Irish brothers, they rarely spoke to each other about such things. A family member in London had introduced Noel to Kate; he had been seeing her for just a few weeks before they were both killed.

It was nearly three months before Noel's body was brought home, after the police released it. The family decided on a closed coffin because of the widespread interest in how Noel had died. Although his face was not injured, they could not bear the idea of people coming to the funeral home to stare at him.

'What really happened?' people would ask Liam Neville, when they did broach the subject. 'Fuck off. It's none of your business,' he felt like saying. He never did say it. 'I don't want to talk about it,' was his usual response.

Alongside the unthinking and casual cruelties, there was genuine kindness shown. In the parish, friends and those closest to the family provided a real support to the Nevilles. In London, where the extended family was involved in amateur soccer, a memorial game was held in Noel's name every year for a decade. Dinner dances were held in London to raise funds to help the family.

After the funeral, Noel was buried beside his father.

Then there was a seven-month wait for the trial. Compared to the Irish courts British murder trials are held relatively quickly after the event, especially in a case such as this one where the perpetrator was found at the scene of the killing and confessed everything.

Tommy Neville went to the trial to represent the family. Margaret and Liam stayed away. It would have been too painful to relive Noel's last moments all over again in a courtroom away from home.

Tobutt pleaded not guilty to murder and his defence team offered a plea bargain. He would plead guilty to manslaughter on the grounds of diminished responsibility. The British Central Criminal Court accepted the deal.

The court heard that Tobutt had pretended to go to work on the late shift that night, but parked his car nearby and hid in the garage of the house in the comfortable suburb of Pinner, north-west London.

According to the account given in court, Tobutt heard his wife talking to Noel about their marriage and flew into a rage. When police arrived after neighbours alerted them, the electronic engineer told them, 'I have killed them. I have killed them.' Noel Neville and Kate Tobutt between them had suffered more than fifty stab wounds.

Tobutt's defence counsel Conrad Seagroatt QC told the trial: 'This was a marriage lacking mutual love and had been for some time, perhaps even from the beginning.'

Without anyone to tell another side of the story, the court was told that the Tobutts had had a turbulent ten-year marriage; that Leslie Tobutt was told constantly by his wife that he was too passive and ineffectual.

The prosecution said Tobutt was obsessively interested in his wife's movements. He had rigged up baby monitors and a crude tube system in his garage to eavesdrop on her telephone conversations.

On 7 September 1992, Judge Kenneth Machin jailed Leslie Tobutt for seven years. The judge said the killer had been suffering from abnormality of mind at the time of the 'grave' killings.

'I sentence you on the basis that there were faults on both sides of this marriage and there was evidence of provocation,' the judge said.

Liam Neville does not understand how two lives can equal seven years. The idea that his brother's death was deemed to have resulted from 'faults on both sides' of a marriage diminishes the Neville family's loss to a footnote.

For his family, Noel's death had an almost surreal quality. At one remove from it in Ireland, his death in London was like the kind of thing that happened in a TV script or crime fiction.

The family of Kate Tobutt wrote to Margaret Neville to sympathise with her about her loss. They offered to meet Margaret. In hindsight it was a generous gesture – both mothers had lost someone thanks to Leslie Tobutt's 'abnormality of mind'. At the time Margaret Neville did not have the heart to get in touch with them.

They did not blame Kate Tobutt for putting Noel in harm's way. Any anger that punctured their numbness was sparked by the press.

For his own part, Liam ploughed himself into work. His exams, part of his training to be a psychiatric nurse, were looming. He was under pressure to pull himself together, to cope and get on with his life. But arriving back in Ireland immediately after his brother's death, he crashed his car on the way to work.

The shock and circumstances of the killing meant that he was unable to talk to his family about what had happened to Noel. Then, six years after Noel's death, Margaret was diagnosed with cancer. Six months later she had died, at the age of just fifty-eight. The four remaining brothers had now lost both parents and their eldest sibling.

In 1997, Liam had to telephone Victim Support in Britain to find out the fate of his brother's killer. They were able to tell him that Tobutt had been released. He had served his sentence and was a free man.

Liam Neville has not focused his mind on Leslie Tobutt. Because he did not go to the trial he never saw him in the flesh. They could pass on the street without recognising each other. There are times when he does wonder about the murder. Questions rattle around about the reality of his brother's death. How it could be humanly possible to do what Tobutt did, to physically stab two people to death? Whom did he kill first? Did the other person know they were going to die as they watched the first victim being stabbed?

Police told the family that Tobutt had been in the British Army. He was a fit, strong man. In court he was a model citizen with no previous convictions. But at the end of the trial the Nevilles were left shocked and appalled. What value did the seven-year sentence place on the two lives that Leslie Tobutt took?

Noel Neville had had a lot of living to do. He was an innocent man who instinctively trusted people. He exuded a warmth that would gather a crowd around him in the pub whenever he was home. Although he was the eldest, he was not the sort of big brother who came over all serious around his younger brothers.

Liam remembers him as a young man who just lived life and enjoyed himself. He took nothing very seriously. He was, in every respect, a man in the prime of his life. Whenever he was home there was a buzz about the place. Everyone in the locality knew him. He was too young to die.

His death and the way that it was reported reduced him to bit-player in a grubby tabloid story – the Irish bricklayer in London in the wrong place at the wrong time. Liam Neville was shocked at what he saw as a lack of respect and sensitivity towards his family's privacy.

By his own admission Liam Neville has buried his feelings about his brother's murder. Yet more than a decade after Noel's death, Liam's professional life is spent dealing with issues of sudden and traumatic death. In 1997 he approached Victim Support about doing some volunteer work with families whose lives had been turned upside down by murder in the way that his had.

The Irish office of Victim Support was set up in 1985 by former garda Derek Nally. A registered charity, the organisation receives State funding – in the year 2000 Victim Support received £1 million from the Department of Justice, Equality and Law Reform. The organisation has forty branches and some 500 volunteers. According to the organisation, it has a sixfold role: support, advocacy, representation, liaison, lobbying and promotion of victims' rights.

In 1993, Bray man Ciaran Bishop and clinical psychologist John Donohoe were instrumental in setting up the Family of Murder Victims (FMV) group within Victim Support. The group provides one-to-one emotional support from trained volunteers. Twenty volunteers work around the country, at the Victim Support centre in Limerick and a therapy group in Dublin. The organisation provides volunteers who accompany family members to a trial, giving them a familiar face and someone to lean on during the dreadful ordeal. In 1998 Liam Neville became chairman of the FMV support group.

Since 2000, Liam Neville has worked with the North Western Health Board as a suicide professional. He deals with schools and teachers, helping them to cope with the aftermath of teenage suicides.

Through Victim Support and the FMV group he has met other families who have been through the experience of suddenly and violently losing a loved one. At one meeting the mother of a teenager who had been murdered spoke movingly and powerfully about the position in which a victim's family finds themselves. They were 'voiceless, powerless and faceless', the mother said.

Her words would be echoed in March 2004 when Mary Murphy, whose teenage son Brian was kicked to death outside Club Anabel in south Dublin in August 2000, addressed the Dublin Circuit Criminal Court.

The trial of four young men accused of the killing led to a tidal wave of publicity. All the elements were there to encourage media interest. For example, there were the affluent backgrounds of the men, including past pupils of Ireland's most famous fee-paying school, Blackrock College. But although the case was covered in much more detail than killings of other young men, the same story was at its heart – two parents, Denis and Mary Murphy, who had lost a son.

Mary Murphy told the court that she had felt under attack in the courtroom in the course of the seven-week trial. Even the seating arrangement reinforced this view. In front of them sat the prosecution barristers and solicitor. 'Beside them were the defence barristers and their solicitors. The media and the accused were also present. All of these people had a voice. Brian and our family, I felt, had no voice. That was why I felt surrounded and under attack.'

Mary Murphy's words received huge attention at the end of the lengthy trial. For some of the families of murder victims, it was the first time anyone seemed to listen to the concerns of a victim's relatives.

'I was going to describe the emptiness in my heart and in my home, about the weeks and months afterwards when I prayed that I would die too, about the anger I felt towards God because I felt He could have stopped this,' Mary Murphy told the court. 'The delay in the trial process added hugely to our pain.'

She went on to paint a vivid picture of her boy, an impulsive, lively teenager who loved and was loved by his family. Her full submission is carried as the last chapter of this book.

The Department of Justice responded to the reaction to the case by saying it was going to re-examine the Charter for Victims' Rights.

The first version of the charter, a document setting down minimum standards with which the various agencies of the

State should treat victims of crime, was published with little fanfare in 1997, under the watch of Fine Gael Justice Minister Nora Owen. Two years later her successor, Fianna Fáil Justice Minister John O'Donoghue, who had generally enjoyed a higher profile, launched another version of the charter with a lengthy speech at Dublin Castle.

'Each and every member of the public is entitled to a standard of service from the state agencies which, after all, are funded either directly or indirectly by the taxpayer,' O'Donoghue said.

'As a crime victim, the treatment you receive afterwards cannot make up for what you and your family may have suffered at the hands of a perpetrator. This is the case irrespective of the nature of the offence.

'A primary aim of this charter is to ensure that victims receive the best possible treatment following a crime and to ensure that in no way are the effects of the crime exacerbated by any failing on behalf of the State agencies involved in the subsequent investigative, prosecution, court, or other processes.'

The forty measures in the charter included the appointment of national victim liaison officers within the Garda Síochána and the Irish Prison Service. The commitment had been made to appoint liaison officers in the force to deal specifically with the families of murder victims. The contents of victim impact statements would now be taken into account in the consideration of early release for an offender. Procedures were put in place to notify victims of the release of an offender.

O'Donoghue ended on a strong note: 'I must emphasise that this charter is not, in any sense, an aspirational document. It places real obligations on each of the parties involved not only to maintain standards but to continue to improve them.'

Four years later, the Garda Policing Plan for 2003 stated that ninety-four percent of people who had been victims of crime said they had received no referral from gardaí to Victim Support. The force has appointed victim liaison officers, but none trained in the highly specialist area of dealing with murder victims' families. In the Garda Policing Plan for 2003, it was stated that the training for this important and highly sensitive role was still at the development stage in the Garda College.

A search for a copy of the Charter for Victims' Rights on the Department of Justice website leads to plenty of press releases and speeches, but no easily accessible document that can be read by victims seeking to identify their rights. The recent history of the State's response to the needs of the families of murder victims has been high on promises and low on delivery.

At the time of writing, working out of the Victim Support headquarters, Liam Neville and his fellow volunteers and colleagues are putting together a group of families of murder victims to form an expert lobby panel. Their aim is to campaign for changes in the system to ease the ordeal of families. The issues are broad and varied, some of them more complex than others.

Meetings of the Family of Murder Victims (FMV) groups have been at times difficult and challenging for all concerned. In the small room at the headquarters on Arran Quay the enormously raw emotion and grief of people has spilled into anger and criticism.

Some of the changes the FMV group are lobbying for are simple, like the provision of travel and accommodation expenses for families attending a murder trial. One family who had made contact with Victim Support was forced to travel many miles by train every day to get to a trial, returning every evening to their rural home, because they could not afford accommodation in Dublin.

There are issues regarding the role of the media – the casual use of a file photograph, or the publication of a photograph of a victim alongside a shot of a perpetrator, can upset a family terribly.

The FMV service wants to see the use of victim impact reports made mandatory in murder trials. The statement is usually seen as a tool for sentencing, but in a murder trial the mandatory sentence of life is handed down on conviction. The FMV group argue that allowing a family to give the court a statement about the effects of the murder on them would give them a sense of being included in the trial process. It would also allow them to give a fitting tribute to the victim at the centre of the whole trial.

Interaction between the family and the barrister for the prosecution is another thorny issue, with the FMV wanting a pre-trial meeting to be held, where the family would receive some kind of briefing on how the trial will be run. In recent years Victim Support had come to an agreement with the Bar Council that these pre-trial meetings would go ahead. In practice, however, they do not always happen.

Then there is the small insult of the death certificate. The sum of 06.98 is charged by registrars of deaths, based at health board buildings around the country, for the issuing of a death certificate. The payment is requested from everyone, even in the case of families whose loved one was murdered. With an average annual murder rate of fifty, the cost to the State of waiving this fee in the case of a murder would be just 0350 a year, a miniscule drop in the ocean of State spending on the criminal justice system.

Vital public health support services, like counselling, are still lacking for people bereaved by murder. There is no publicly funded, coherent counselling service available for families in the aftermath of a murder.

The path to a counsellor's office is usually taken by bereaved relatives on their own initiative, seeking out help when they find it difficult to continue to function. The normal route is a referral through a GP to a private counsellor. Treatment can range from occasional sessions with someone who has done a short counsellor-training course, to regular and expensive consultations with a psychiatrist or psychologist.

The health boards offer counselling for the bereaved, but their waiting lists are very long. This is a particularly acute problem in relation to children. Waiting lists for children awaiting bereavement counselling can be between three to six months long. Six months is a sizeable time in anyone's calendar, and can be like a lifetime to a child. The FMV group wants children bereaved by murder to receive priority on the waiting lists.

Another major problem is caused by a different waiting list. The backlog of cases before the Central Criminal Court, where all murder cases must be tried, has been highlighted by Judge Paul Carney. In recent years High Court judges have been thinner on the ground than normal, taken up as they are with tribunals and reports commissioned by government.

In July 2003 the Central Criminal Court sat outside Dublin, in a Limerick courthouse, for the first time in its history. The Limerick court was set up to hear rape and murder trials for the following two years.

The move was made to free up space in the Four Courts. The Courts Service stated that average waiting times for a trial to come to the Central Criminal Court had already been reduced from two years to fourteen months, following the assignment of four High Court judges to permanent duties in the Central Criminal Court.

But a speech by Supreme Court Judge Susan Denham in March 2004 highlighted that something more is required than just a reorganisation of the existing system. Justice Denham outlined stark figures on the number of judges in Ireland.

With just 120 judges in the country, in Ireland there are fewer members of the judiciary per head of population than in other European countries or in the common law jurisdictions of New Zealand, Australia and Canada, she said. For every 100,000 people in the country there are just three judges. 'The next time you are concerned about getting a case on, or wait as a court sits late to deal with a long list, consider the current situation. One hundred and twenty people comprise the third branch of government in Ireland,' she said.

The families of murder victims do not comprise a strong lobby group in the scheme of power politics in the State. As a group they are people suffering severe emotional distress, compounded by overwhelming feelings of powerlessness. They are not a homogenous collection of people; not everyone will have the same priorities or concerns. Murder crosses rural and urban divides as well as class and cultural ones.

It is a truism that a society can be judged by how it treats its most vulnerable citizens. In the aftermath of a murder even the most powerful citizens are reduced to the role of bystanders in a drama played out as the State investigates and then, sometimes, prosecutes the murderer.

LIFE SENTENCE

For Liam Neville, the murder of his brother in London has brought him, more than a decade later, to the centre of the issue of how the Irish authorities deal with murder. The work may bring some healing. To campaign is to do something, to focus on making some kind of difference or regaining some control.

To lose a loved one to murder is an unthinkable prospect for anyone. The situation that exists at present whereby the State adds insult to the worst injury life can deal a person is a mess that has to be addressed.

Chapter 13

Where is my baby in all of this?

Brian Murphy was kicked and beaten to death outside Club Anabel, a nightclub at the Burlington Hotel in south Dublin, in August 2000.

Four young men were charged in connection with the killing of the eighteen-year-old student. The trial, which began in January 2004, lasted over six weeks.

In February 2004 three of the men – Dermot Laide (twenty-two) of Rossvale, Castleblaney, County Monaghan; Sean Mackey (twenty-three) of South Park, Foxrock, Dublin 18; and Desmond Ryan (twenty-three) of Cunningham Road, Dalkey, County Dublin – were convicted of violent disorder in relation to the attack on Brian Murphy. One of them, Dermot Laide, was also convicted of manslaughter.

Laide was sentenced to four years for the manslaughter and a concurrent two years for the violent disorder. Mackey was jailed for two years and Ryan received a nine-month sentence on the violent disorder convictions. All three men have lodged appeals.

At the Circuit Criminal Court on Monday, 8 March 2004, Brian Murphy's mother Mary made a submission to the court describing her experience of the murder trial and paying tribute to her late son.

This is what she said:

> I am here for Brian. This is the most nerve-wracking thing I have ever done. I'm doing it also for myself because I have been forced to keep silent for so long. But my real motivation in taking the stand here today comes from my deep love for my son.
>
> The love that one has for one's child is primal. It's the type of love where you would put your own safety at risk. It is the only comparison I have for the love that God has for us.
>
> I wasn't there when Brian was savagely kicked and beaten to death. If I had been there you would not have succeeded in your quest to attack my baby because you would have had to kill me first.
>
> I spent a lot of my time over the past week preparing a text for this impact statement. It contained details and a description of how I felt in the immediate aftermath of Brian's death, how we were told not to touch his body in case we would destroy evidence. There were details I wanted to share about Brian's wake, his funeral and his burial. When I read it over in preparation for today, it sounded so hollow. When I asked myself why did I feel this way, the feeling came that apart from the judge and my own close family and friends the rest of those listening to me probably didn't want to know. When I thought about that I realised how much I have felt under attack in this courtroom over the past seven weeks.
>
> I will try and outline why I have felt this way.
>
> Firstly, when I woke up the next morning still thinking about this, I noticed as I lay in the bed that I had my two arms tightly over my face and that there was huge tension in my whole body.
>
> In a strange way I felt that there was an uncanny resemblance between Brian's predicament in his final moments and my feelings of being surrounded by people whom I felt didn't want to know about our tragedy.
>
> Just thinking about our family's seating position in Court 23 helps me to further enhance what I'm talking about.
>
> In front of us were seated the prosecution barristers, and solicitor. Beside them were the defence barristers and their

solicitors. The media and the accused were also present. All of these people had a voice. Brian and our family, I felt, had no voice. That was why I felt surrounded and under attack.

I would like to describe how I felt about these various parties.

First of all we heard the prosecution, who don't represent Brian, but who act on behalf of the people of Ireland and therefore represent the State. I felt the rules governing how they were allowed to argue the case to be so restrictive. To me the evidence of some witnesses was confusing and contradictory, yet the prosecution was not able to recall these witnesses for clarification.

Then we have the defence teams. The main effect that the defence had on me was that I felt I was being brainwashed into thinking that what happened to Brian was somehow his own fault. The repetition of evidence over and over again somehow desensitises everyone to the reality of what happened to Brian.

The summing up of the defence tried to paint all the defendants in such a wonderful light, that it was a tragedy for them to have to be sitting here as defendants at all. Are you allowed, in summing up, to blatantly contradict a scientific witness, such as Dr Harbison, who stated that Brian consumed less than twice the legal limit of alcohol permitted when driving a car? This means that Brian consumed between three and four pints on the night in question. In the summing up there was a suggestion that he consumed twice that amount.

Then there is the media. I think the message abroad from the media is that the tragedy of our family and those of the accused is in some way comparable. The opinion of the general public seems to suggest that any of their children could have been involved in a similar attack. It was a tragedy for these guys. The headline in one Sunday broadsheet epitomises what I'm saying, where Brian is described as 'The Luckless Murphy'. This suggests that poor Brian was just unfortunate to be in the wrong place at the wrong time.

The biggest fault I have become aware of as I have read some media is that they are quoting as fact something that has been alleged, and are using that to back up their own agenda. This has the cumulative effect for me of diminishing Brian as a human being. I would just like to clarify that I have felt that direct evidence quoted by the reporters which speak directly about the evidence as presented before the jury has been, in my opinion, for the most part accurate. But remember, this is only evidence. People who swear before God to tell the truth, the whole truth and nothing but the truth don't necessarily do that.

And, finally, you have those convicted of their part in Brian's killing, who have attempted to deny and minimise their part in Brian's death.

So, maybe now you can understand why I could not share my innermost feelings about my beautiful darling son to a listenership such as this.

So, I don't intend to go into any great detail about how if felt to watch Brian, as he lay dead on a hospital bed with his two front teeth smashed; or about the long wait before his body was brought back home in a coffin to us; what it was like to watch my child lie in a coffin with my rosary beads wrapped around his hands and Brona's private letter to him lying on top of his body.

I have an abiding memory of so many candles lighting all day and all night in the room with him. I am not going to tell you about the prayers of forgiveness, which we composed ourselves, and which we brought before God at Brian's funeral Mass. I won't attempt to describe the devastation I felt at Mount Jerome crematorium, as the curtain went across Brian's coffin to the music of Brian's favourite song, 'November Rain', or about the box of ashes I carried to his grave.

I was going to describe the emptiness in my heart and in my home, about the weeks and months afterwards when I prayed that I would die too, about the anger I felt towards God because I felt He could have stopped this. The delay in the trial process added hugely to our pain.

So where is my baby in all of this? I can't find him. He's lost. I'm lost. All my family and friends are lost too.

Where is my pride and joy, my full of confidence child, my crazy, exuberant, full of cheer, larger than life child. My naive, far from perfect child, who did some silly things and some fabulous things.

On the basis that the judge does want to know who Brian was I will attempt to introduce you to this dehumanised, by the trial process, Brian Murphy. Actions speak louder than words. Anyone who saw the video of Brian interacting with his little brother on TV should be able to see the vitality, the warmth that was in him as he rubbed the top of Robert's head after he kissed him and used the words, 'I love you too, Baby.'

Here is my humble attempt to describe Brian. Anyone who knew him would say that he was a free spirit who was larger than life. He had a special charm that drew people to him. He was eighteen, remember. He had still a lot of maturing to do both physically, emotionally and mentally. He was highly intelligent. His exuberant personality refused to be quashed.

As a person, Brian had time for everyone. He labelled no-one. He had so many friends from all schools and our local soccer club. His friends came from every walk of life and every background. He was not an adopted Clongownian. He liked people for who they were and nothing else. What schools people attended was irrelevant to him.

He was a brilliant listener. He made you feel you were important to him. He was so open. There was no pretence, what you saw and heard was the real him, warts and all. He was an individual, with his own views. He was a leader. His sense of humour was second to none. To remember him is to smile. He would introduce humour into the everyday, the banal. The spirit that was Brian was manifested in his appreciation of the finer things of life.

At his funeral Mass a young lady told a story about Brian from the altar. How he brought her into the National Gallery to show her, in his own words, the best painting ever. It was a painting called 'The Opening of the Sixth Seal', the theme of which was taken from the Book of Revelations in the Bible. It was painted with a black background, with a red sun, and orange and red flashes of lightning. He was fascinated by it.

He loved poetry. I vividly remember the days prior to his Leaving Cert English exam of him showing off how he could recite every poem on the course, even though this wasn't necessary for the exam.

He loved mountains. His favourite holiday was one we spent camping in the Alps. We have put a picture of Mount Fuji on his memorial bookmark because that is a place he longed to visit. In a book where he had read about Mount Fuji, called *The Natural Wonders of the World*, Mount Fuji is described as a place of pilgrimage and a sacred place, the reason being that its coned peak goes above the clouds, and there is an air of Heaven and Earth coming together at its peak.

Dr Harbison said that Brian had a slightly enlarged heart. Clare said to me afterwards that was a good description of Brian; that is, that he had such a big heart. Stories of Brian's big heart abound. The one which sticks in my mind happened during the summer before Brian's death.

He came with me and Robert to visit my mother, who was suffering from Alzheimer's disease. She was in a nursing home in Bray. We walked to the seafront with her, with Brian holding her hand. We sat on a bench at the seafront with her. Brian gave her a cigarette, and we laughed as she tapped the ash in the way she would have prior to her illness.

Brian put his arm around her and said, 'Gran, I'm sorry I haven't been to see you in a while,' and he started to cry. She did not understand a word he was saying. He then went to the seashore with Robert to show him how to skim stones on water.

He was delighted at Robert's success in doing this and gave me the thumbs up from the water's edge. Robert remembers this day also.

There is a story of him bringing home, unbeknownst to me, a man who was down on his luck to our home and him cooking one of his specialities for him.

To me he was my best mate. I had completed first year as a mature student in UCD in the faculty of social science. I found studying for the exams really tough. Brian was there for me with his encouragement to keep at it. To his delight I passed my exams. During that summer, I worked as a social care worker with a young girl who was a heroin addict.

I found the work emotionally draining and Brian was a ready listener when I described to him what life was like for this young girl.

What I really miss most of all about Brian is the fun we had together. My best memory of this is our day together on his eighteenth birthday. We went into town and bought his present, having travelled to every shop in town. I will never forget the camaraderie there was between us as we chatted over lunch in a restaurant chosen by him.

He told one of his friends, speaking of me, 'Mary understands me.' I am so glad that he said this as it gives me huge consolation.

How do I convey how Brian's death has affected me? The pain I felt was physical. I could not shed a single tear, which would have been an outlet for some of the pain. The pain was one of shock, numbness and grief which had no outlet because I could not cry. In time, with the feeling of anger came the tears, which at least gave some release to the pain.

I have and will continue to have great difficulty letting myself feel the sadness. Devastation is more the word to describe it. I have to blank that out. This will never go away and it is something I have to try to accept.

Then I think of what it was like for Brian and his final moments. What was the horror and terror like for him? He must have been pleading in his mind, 'Will somebody help me.'

This talk about Brian's group. What group? If Brian was with a group he would still be alive, because they would have come to his defence. The boasting and cheering are scary, like we have gone back to the dark ages. Words like manslaughter and violent disorder make killing sound respectable. This I find nauseating.

I wonder what legal jargon would be used if Brian hadn't died but was left brain-damaged, with the suffering that would have been for him and us. Denis and I have lost our beautiful son's future – his maturing, his becoming more sensible as he got older. But the biggest thing we have lost out on is his sense of fun.

Robert was six years old when his big brother, whom he loved, was snatched from him. Robert started to play matches for his football club a year after Brian died. Brian would have been his number one supporter on the sideline, offering all sorts of advice to his little brother. Denis said just after Robert was born that he was looking forward to the day when Brian, Robert and himself would attend matches together. This never happened. I imagine the slagging there would have been between them over premiership results, Brian being a Spurs supporter and Robert a Liverpool supporter. All Robert has left of Brian is his picture which he has pasted to his bedside locker, a teddy Brian gave him, and an old Spurs shirt of Brian's, which Robert sleeps on at night when he is feeling particularly sad. Robert goes through phases of sadness. It usually happens at night when he cries and says, 'I miss Brian.' I hate this loss for Robert more than anything.

Brona told me of an evening when he arrived home, when she was babysitting Robert and he walked in and said to her, 'Brona, you know I love you.' This coming from an eighteen-year-old boy to his fourteen-year-old sister shows what a special person he was. There are sixteen months between Clare and Brian. They were like peas in a pod, doing everything together.

What effect has the trial had on me? I'm back to when Brian died. That we should be forced to revisit it after three-and-a-half years is inhuman. The shock, the anger, the sadness are back, and along with these is fear which must be present as a result of hearing the details of what happened to Brian. I wonder will I ever feel safe again, because the way the justice system works makes me think that we live in a very unsafe society.

I wanted questions answered by coming to this trial every day. The way I see it, there was no fight when Brian was killed. There was a concerted savage attack, where he was surrounded and kicked to death.

I feel brutalised by this trial process. The quest for the truth becomes a battle between two sides caught in a game, each side trying to win points. Brian gets lost. Brian becomes the object in the red shirt. There are some phrases that are ingrained in my mind and will be with me for the rest of my life:

'We got him good.' Other witnesses used another version of this which I prefer not to repeat.

'This is great craic.'

'Behaving like animals.' As a lover of animals I find that remark insulting to animals.

'He fell flat on his face with no arms to save him.'

'I started all this.'

'The wave of feet.'

'I couldn't put faces with feet,' by witnesses who knew the accused.

The new shoes kicking him. The big-headed guy who walked from the group kicking Brian.

'I heard his head snap, crack and I felt it go soft.'

I used to think that whoever did this will have to live with it for the rest of their lives, which is why I prayed for them and their families at Brian's funeral and at subsequent anniversary Masses.

After attending this trial and hearing what I have heard, I don't think that any more. They just want to get off.

If they had a conscience and if they were really sorry for what they have done, they would tell the whole truth about what has happened, own up and take the consequences.

Truth is lost here. Brian is lost here. I am lost here. I have agonised over forgiveness over these past years since Brian's death, how I couldn't find it in my heart to forgive. I wasn't going to pretend to forgive, it had to come from my heart.

From the way this whole case has gone I am clear on one thing. I cannot contemplate forgiveness until I know the truth and those responsible for Brian's death have acknowledged their part in it and make known the part others played in his killing.

The anger I felt mounting as the trial progressed was all about what I have just said – that nobody was owning up. The way I see it, that is the only way of getting on with the rest of your lives. There is no way of hiding from the truth. It demands to be seen and heard.

On considering this issue for myself, I was reminded of the account in the Bible of the crucifixion of Jesus, where the two criminals were on crosses on each side of him. One said to Jesus, 'If you are a king, you save us.' The one on his other side said, 'Leave him alone, he has done no wrong. We deserve to be here, he doesn't.' Jesus said to this criminal, 'You will be with me today in paradise.' He did not say it to the other one. The man who told the truth won the favour of Jesus.

To conclude, we as a family have to go from here to try and get on with our lives. I know that in time and with God's help, as I move through all the pain that is ahead of me, that I will survive as Brian has survived. I know for Brian that life has changed, not ended. I am not afraid of death any more. I look forward to running into Brian's outstretched arms as he enfolds me in his warm, joyful embrace.

I have a memory which convinces me of Brian's state. Some months after he died I was coming out of a deep sleep when I heard his voice in my head, which just said, 'sorry.'

He had come back to say this word to me. It was a word which I was used to when he was alive. Whenever we had words, which mothers of teenagers often do, he would be heading out afterwards and he'd shout, 'I'll see you, Mum.' Then he'd have qualms of conscience about what had been said and he'd arrive back and say, 'Sorry, Mum,' about whatever the disagreement had been about. I'd say, 'It's okay, Brian,' and he'd head off much happier. The fact that Brian came back and said this word to me is a sign to me that he is still alive.

I am so thankful for the support I get from my husband Denis and my three other children. I hope I can support them also. I am so thankful for the support of the rest of my extended family and for the support of our good, honest, trustworthy, faithful and loving friends.

Can I make an appeal to the media? Please don't misquote me, or quote me out of context. Please, please respect my integrity. It is so hurtful to see yourself misquoted, or the wrong slant put on what you say. If you care in any way about me or Brian and my family please take the time to understand what I'm saying. I feel that the lives of those convicted in connection with Brian's death are not ruined, as some media have said about them. They are not ruined if they can summon up the huge courage that is needed to face the truth.

The truth will set you free.

Reprinted with the kind permission of Mary and Denis Murphy.

MANIFESTO OF RIGHTS OF PEOPLE BEREAVED BY MURDER

Compiled by Victim Support Families of Murder Victims Coordinator, Moe Reynolds

1. Information: A single issue that stands above the rest – the consistent provision of clear and accurate information. A cultural change needs to be encouraged in all statutory and voluntary agencies dealing with people bereaved by murder.

2. Social services and support: Most families are in urgent need of assistance from the social services, from the psychological services, special counselling for children, financial assistance and medical care. Support is needed immediately following the aftermath of a murder, and on a long-term basis.

Immediately after a murder a representative from a social welfare office, health board or counsellor should contact the family to offer support and give information about available services.

Child counselling should be offered immediately after a murder, offered free of charge, available nationwide and if possible provided in the home environment.

The health boards should offer free counselling to all families bereaved by murder on an outreach basis.

A core group of counsellors should be trained to deal with people bereaved by murder.

The support of other families should be established nationally both on a one-to-one basis and in a well-managed group setting.

3. Proper handling of families by the gardaí: The gardaí are key figures and can be in contact with a family for the many years it can take for a case to reach the trial stages.

The news of a murder should always be delivered by an experienced and empathetic member of the force.

Investigating gardaí should explain clearly their role to the family, especially if they are constrained in the amount of information they can share with a family.

The gardaí should actively and continually provide information to families on the investigation process, charging any alleged offender, bail, prosecution, sentencing and release of offenders.

Families should be told of every court hearing so they can decide themselves whether or not to attend.

The family should be told that gardaí are duty-bound to reveal in court anything a family member may have told them in private.

Garda liaison officers need to be trained to support the families and manage their own responses to this difficult and stressful situation.

In cases of a murder overseas, gardaí should keep in contact with the family.

The gardaí need to be up to date on the services provided by Victim Support and how to contact them.

4. The courts: More judges need to be appointed and new court accommodation must be built and in the meantime emergency sessions should be held to clear the backlog.

Families should be kept informed of the exact timing of a trial and kept updated on any rescheduling.

The sentence should fit the crime. Crimes against people should be more severe than a crime against property.

The family should be forewarned when the State Pathologist or any physical evidence is to be introduced during a trial in order to give them the opportunity to leave the court.

Requests by family members to meet prosecuting counsel should be honoured. If there are any procedural reasons why this cannot happen (for example if a family member is to be a witness), then reasons for this should be explained to the family in advance.

During the trial either a garda or a member of the State prosecution team should try to explain the trial process to the family.

A Victim Impact Statement should be mandatory in murder trials. Without it a family feels no notice has been paid to their loss and they have had no say in the proceedings.

5. The media: A lack of courtesy and consideration for the bereaved causes hardship and distress. There are some measures that can alleviate that:

Informing the family of any broadcasts involving the offender or the victim can be done by a phone call from the reporter or producer.

Photographs of the bodies of murder victims should never be published in the newspapers.

Sensitivity should be used when publishing photographs of the victim and the perpetrator alongside each other on the pages of a newspaper.

No photograph of a victim should be published without the family's permission and knowledge.

Stricter standards should be adopted regarding erroneous information published about the victim or the case. Families should have recourse to a complaints procedure.

Gardaí should suggest appointing an appropriate family spokesperson to protect the privacy of the rest of the family.

6. The post mortem and Coroner's Court: Gardaí should always offer the family the opportunity to view the body. The family should be allowed to decide who it is that will formally identify the victim.

Information should be provided to clearly set out the role of the Coroner.

Families attending the Coroner's Court should be acknowledged by the Coroner.

7. Financial and compensation needs: The Department of Justice should earmark a fund to cover the costs of travel and accommodation costs for a family to attend court.

Interim payments should be made by the Criminal Injuries Compensation Tribunal in cases where families are waiting long periods for an inquest to be held.

Assistance should be offered to families applying to the Criminal Injuries Compensation Tribunal in filling in the application form and gathering the appropriate paperwork.

The situation whereby a family is not entitled to compensation if the offender and the victim lived in the same house should be changed. This condition penalises families where the murder was inter-familial or the offender was well-known to the victim.

LIFE SENTENCE

Payments for funeral and other similar bills should be made separately to the main compensation payment.

The state should automatically pay for the funeral and the headstone.

8. Other considerations:
Families should always be informed if:

Any appeals are launched by the offender.

The offender is released on probation.

The accused is released on bail.